DISCARDED

D0938844

115.

Herman and Daphine Rooks
Jerusalem
July 14, 15 + 16, 1978

The Noble Sanctuary

Portrait of a Holy Place in Arab Jerusalem

by
Alistair Duncan

with acknowledgement to
Al Haram al-Sharif by Aref al-Aref

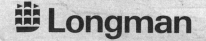 Longman

LONGMAN GROUP LIMITED
London

Associated companies, branches and representatives throughout the world

© Photographs: Middle East Archive (Alistair Duncan) 1972
© Text: Alistair Duncan 1972

All rights reserved. No part of this publication may be reproduced, stored in a retrieval system, or transmitted in any form or by any means, electronic, mechanical, photocopying, recording, or otherwise, without the prior permission of the Copyright owner.

First published 1972

ISBN 0 582 78029 2

Set in Monophoto Univers

ACKNOWLEDGEMENTS
We are grateful to Allen and Unwin Ltd. for permission to reproduce adapted quotations from *The Koran Interpreted* by Arthur Arberry. The author gratefully acknowledges the assistance given to him by the Supreme Awqaf Council of Jordan.
In addition the works of (among others) the following authors have provided valuable reference material: W. F. Albright, K. A. C. Creswell, Sir John Glubb, John Gray, L. H. Grollenberg, Eugène Hoade, Michel Join-Lambert, Flavius Josephus, Kathleen M. Kenyon, Guy Le Strange, Anthony Nutting, Stewart Perowne, Sir Steven Runciman, W. B. Stevenson, M.-J. Stève, A. L. Tibawi, Colin Thubron, Roland de Vaux, Sir Charles Warren and Sir Charles Wilson.

Printed in Great Britain by Jarrold and Sons Ltd, Norwich

It is also dedicated to
the memory of all who
have died in defence of
the Rights of Man
to live and worship in
his own Homeland.
'Surely unto God all
things return home.'
The Holy Qur'an XLII

This book is dedicated
to the memory of
ABD AL-MALIK IBN MARAWAN
(upon whose soul may
God's Mercy remain)
and to all who have
worshipped in Jerusalem
and demonstrated their
faith by the skills of
their hands in
this Holy Place.

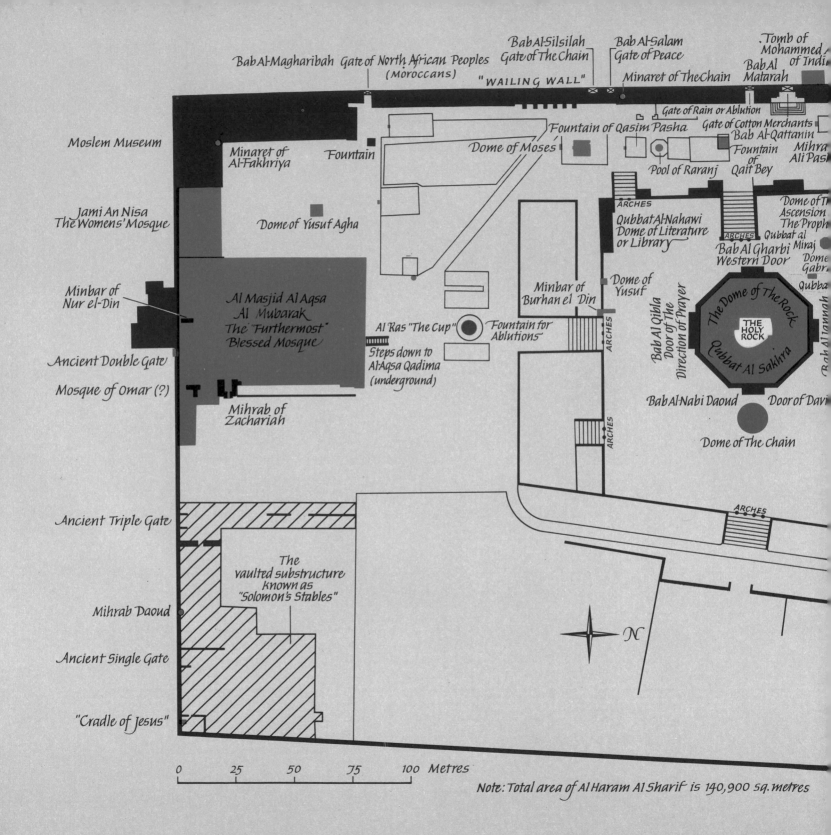

Bab Al-Magharibah Gate of North African Peoples
(Moroccans)

Bab Al-Silsilah
Gate of The Chain

Bab Al-Salam
Gate of Peace

Tomb of
Mohammed
of India

Bab Al
Matarah

"WAILING WALL"

Minaret of The Chain

Moslem Museum

Minaret of
Al-Fakhriya

Fountain

Gate of Rain or Ablution

Fountain of Qasim Pasha

Dome of Moses

Gate of Cotton Merchants

Bab Al-Qattanin

Fountain
of
Qait Bey

Mihra
Ali Pas

Pool of Raranj

Jami An Nisa
The Womens' Mosque

Dome of Yusuf Agha

Qubbat Al-Nahawi
Dome of Literature
or Library

ARCHES

Dome of T
Ascension
The Proph

Qubbat al
Miraj

ARCHES

Bab Al Gharbi
Western Door

Dome
Gabr

Qubba

Minbar of
Nur el-Din

Al Masjid Al Aqsa
Al Mubarak
The "Furthermost"
Blessed Mosque

Minbar of
Burhan el Din

Dome of
Yusuf

Dome of The Rock

Bab Al Qibla
Door of The
Direction of Prayer

Bab Al'annah

Al Ras "The Cup"

Fountain for
Ablutions

THE
HOLY
ROCK

Ancient Double Gate

Mosque of Omar (?)

Steps down to
Al-Aqsa Qadima
(underground)

ARCHES

Qubbat Al Sakhra

Mihrab of
Zachariah

ARCHES

Bab Al-Nabi Daoud

Door of Davi

Dome of The Chain

Ancient Triple Gate

The
vaulted substructure
known as
"Solomon's Stables"

ARCHES

Mihrab Daoud

Ancient Single Gate

N

"Cradle of Jesus"

0   25   50   75   100 Metres

Note: Total area of Al Haram Al Sharif is 140,900 sq. metres

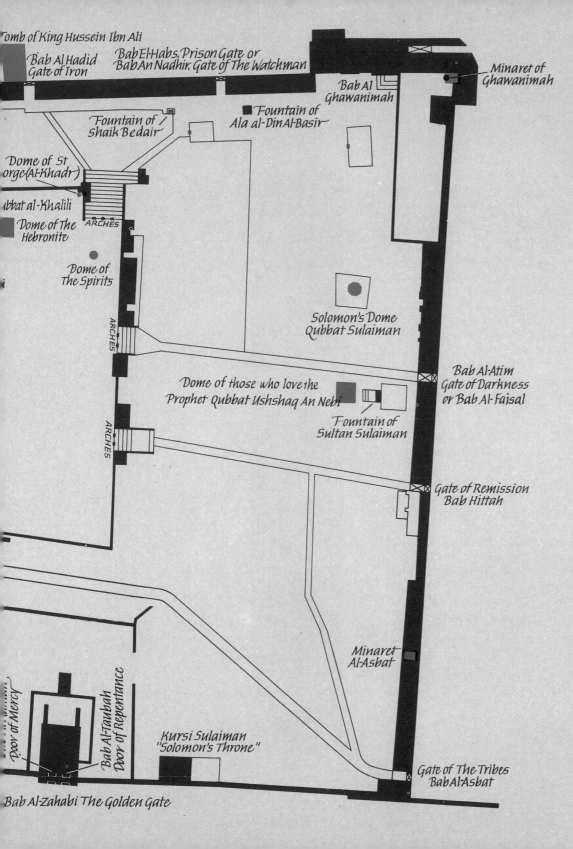

Tomb of King Hussein Ibn Ali

Bab Al Hadid
Gate of Iron

Bab El-Habs, Prison Gate or
Bab An Nadhir, Gate of The Watchman

Minaret of
Ghawanimah

Bab Al
Ghawanimah

Fountain of
Shaik Bedair

Fountain of
Ala al-Din Al-Basir

Dome of St
orge (Al-Khadr)

ubbat al-Khalili

Dome of The
Hebronite

ARCHES

Dome of
The Spirits

Solomon's Dome
Qubbat Sulaiman

ARCHES

Bab Al-Atim
Gate of Darkness
or Bab Al-Faisal

Dome of those who love the
Prophet Qubbat Ushshaq An Nebi

ARCHES

Fountain of
Sultan Sulaiman

Gate of Remission
Bab Hittah

Minaret
Al-Asbat

Door of Mercy

Bab Al-Taubah
Door of Repentance

Kursi Sulaiman
"Solomon's Throne"

Gate of The Tribes
Bab Al-Asbat

Bab Al-Zahabi The Golden Gate

JERUSALEM
The Old City

The Noble Sanctuary

This sketch map is based upon that of
Mr Abder Rahman Rissas of Amman,
Jordan, which itself was drawn from the
survey map prepared by the British
Mandate Government of Palestine.

Colour Guide: the green areas indicate
religious buildings or shrines. The blue
shows the open fountain of Al Kas, and
yellow the area of the Holy Rock
(Sakhra).

Endpapers: an aerial photograph of
Jerusalem by courtesy of the Ministry of
Defence, showing the situation of Al
Haram Al Sharif within the City.
(British Crown Copyright Reserved)

Preface

I first saw Jerusalem from the Mount of Olives. It was late in the afternoon. The sunlight from the west blazed back from the Dome of the Rock and the city shimmered like a crown upon the lion-coloured hills about the Holy City. From that vantage-point one looks down upon history itself. The site emerged from prehistory at the time of the Semitic migration into Palestine. Jewish and Christian tradition says that Abraham prepared to sacrifice his son Isaac upon the Mount of Moriah, which lies opposite across the Kidron valley. Thereafter, Man has raised on this place sacred buildings in reverence to his God. Muslims, however, believe that Abraham's sacrifice was to have been of his eldest son, Ishmael, when he was many miles away near Mecca. Since 691 C.E.* this site, the epicentre of a turbulent city where faith and belief have too often been distorted into zealous fury and sectarian persecution, has been marked by a building of sublime beauty. Set upon an open and level space, the Dome of the Rock is as magnificent a tribute to the glory of God as can be seen anywhere in the world. Nearby is the site of Solomon's Temple and of its Herodian successor. Nearby, too, the Aqsa Mosque marks the staging-point of the Prophet Muhammad's miraculous night journey from Mecca to Jerusalem.

It was my good fortune to spend many hours in the Noble Sanctuary with Aref al-Aref, a distinguished authority on this Holy Place of Islam. Born in Jerusalem and twice elected as its mayor, he has written many books, including a concise history of these buildings and structures which together are called Al Haram al-Sharif. Anyone attempting to portray this place and its history must acknowledge the value of Aref's work to those who visit and study there.

I hope that this folio of photographs and the accompanying text will give the reader some pleasure in the art, craftsmanship and beauty of the Noble Sanctuary, and that sufficient interest may be aroused to stimulate sympathy and understanding for all who have lived and aspired to peace within the walls of Jerusalem.

* C.E., Common Era = Anno Domini.

Springtime. The Dome of the Rock seen from the Mount of Olives.

Introduction

In 629 C.E. the empire of Byzantium was in decline in the East. The Emperor Heraclius had rescued the True Cross from the Persians, who had captured it when they took Jerusalem in 614. He returned it in triumph to the Holy City.

But time was running out. By 636 the Arab forces were moving out from Arabia. On 20th August, by the banks of the Yarmuk river which joins the Jordan just below the Sea of Galilee, the Byzantine army was crowded together, far outnumbering its Arab opponents. The day dawned hot, with a brazen sky. Soon a searing wind whipped the sand into a fury. Khaled Ibn al-Walid, commanding a far smaller force, drove into his enemies' ranks from out of the sun and with the terrible wind behind him. The battle raged for three days. The few Byzantine survivors withdrew to Constantinople, never to return.

Who were these new conquerors? What inspiration led them?

We must go back sixty-five years to 571. In Mecca was born a boy called Muhammad, who was destined to be hailed by his followers as the last great Prophet of God. As he grew up he worked for a merchant for whom he travelled along the trade route nearly as far north as Damascus. He became disillusioned with the society which surrounded him: with the multiple idolatries of Arabia, with the exclusiveness of the Jews and what he believed to be certain distorted texts in their Bible, and with particular developments of ritual and doctrine within the Christian Church. But he agreed that both Jew and Christian had their sacred book and a share of the Truth revealed by God. Like other great prophets before him, he saw hope for the future of the community only in a disciplined life and in the recognition and worship of the one true God by its individual members. On his death in 632, such was his influence that his followers had overcome all local resistance and, though poor, were left with a new dignity and sense of personal responsibility. Their growing numbers accepted Muhammad's new code of social justice, corresponding in contemporary terms to a charter of human rights. All this, together with the ritual of daily prayers, formed the strength of the Faith, which remains to this day, binding together all who embrace Islam.

Holy tradition has it that during his lifetime and in the course of his ministry Muhammad received direct divine inspiration and a series of instructions from God. These revelations constitute the book of the Holy Qur'an.

The Noble Sanctuary viewed from Mount Scopus (north-east) across the Kidron Valley.

One chapter (Sura 17) describes his miraculous journey by night from Mecca to Jerusalem:

Glory be to him, who carried his servant by night
from the Holy Mosque to the Farthest Mosque
the precincts of which We have blessed,
that We might show him some of Our signs.
He is All-hearing and All-seeing.

On this journey Muhammad was accompanied by the archangel Gabriel. On reaching Jerusalem he prayed along with prophets of the past at the place where the Dome over the Holy Rock now stands. He was then taken to the sacred rock, from which he ascended to heaven by a stairway of light. After being conducted by Gabriel through all the seven heavens, he at last stood in the Divine Presence to receive instructions for himself and for his followers. He returned the way he had come, down the staircase of light, reaching Mecca before dawn.

To the Rock at Jerusalem the Prophet Muhammad had come at God's command. It was towards Jerusalem, holy to the followers of Islam since the time of Abraham and the later prophets, Moses, Solomon, El Khadr (Elijah) and Jesus, that Muslims first directed their prayers. The change of the *qibla* (direction of prayer) occurred while the Prophet was praying near Medina. The revelation which prompted him to make the change is set out in the second *sura* (chapter) of the Qur'an, and thereby established the Ka'aba of Mecca as the religious centre to which all Muslims have turned to pray ever since, just as it had been in previous times and prehistory for the people of Arabia.

This briefly is the religious significance of Jerusalem for six hundred million Muslims, within and beyond the Arab world.

The Golden Gate (Al Bab Al Zahabi) and the eastern walls of Sulaiman the Magnificent seen from the Garden of Gethsemane (Kidron Valley).

The Background of History

Ten portions of beauty, gave God to the world; nine to Jerusalem and one for the remainder.
Ten portions of sorrow, gave God to the world; nine to Jerusalem and one for the rest of mankind.

It was about 3000 B.C.E. that an Arabic people known as Kanaanis moved out of central Arabia to settle on the high plateau overlooking the fertile coastal plains of Canaan. They were the forebears of the Canaanites, of whom the earliest known records are from Egypt. The so-called Tel el-Amarna letters or tablets record messages to the then Pharaoh Totmoses I asking for protection against raiding Semitic nomads. Their fortified town was known as Orosalem after a Canaanite god. It is also referred to in history as Warwa Salem and Yaro Salem, names which may either have an Aramaic origin, or come from a later Babylonian source.

We know with certainty that excavations carried out on Mount Ophel, below the present city and adjacent to and south of Al Haram al-Sharif, have revealed an Early Bronze Age settlement about 2600 B.C.E. and a Middle Bronze Age town encompassed by a massive wall about 1800 B.C.E., set on the hillside above the Gihon spring in the Kidron valley.

The Late Bronze Age saw the city inhabited by Jebusites of Canaanite extraction. At that time (about 1400 B.C.E.) the city was known as Jebus or Jebusi and is frequently so mentioned in the Old Testament. It is curious that the site did not extend to the top of the hill. One explanation could be that this highest part was already devoted to religious or cultic rites: in effect a holy place for the Canaanites.

About 1200 B.C.E. the Hebrew invasion of Canaan under the leadership of Joshua (Moses' successor) began with the fording of the Jordan river and the destruction of Jericho. By the time of Joshua's death most of the country had been conquered in a campaign of great bloodshed and destruction lasting many years. Only Jebus held out, marooned in its strong defensive location. Finally Joshua's successor David sent a commando led by Joab to infiltrate the city by climbing up the well shaft from the Gihon spring beneath its walls.

Thus, about 1000 B.C.E. David established his capital for the federation of the tribes of Judah and Israel in Canaan together with its indigenous inhabitants. Nearly one hundred years later, on the death of David's son Solomon, the federation broke up. Separate kingdoms of Judah and Israel were formed, with Jerusalem (Jebus) and Samaria as their respective capitals. The Egyptians moved north to fill the power vacuum caused by the weakness of the new states and Jerusalem was sacked. Israel on the other hand built up its

The Golden Gate seen from within the walls.

associations with the rich trading people of Phoenicia. Stability and prosperity were enhanced by the marriage of Israel's King Ahab to Jezebel, daughter of the King of Tyre, and by the acceptance of the northern pantheon of deities, notably Baal, as the official gods. However, a peasant revolt led by the prophet Elijah (El Khadr) brought an end to the gross inequalities and injustices of this corrupt regime. Soon afterwards, Baal was introduced as an official god into Judah. But, with the subsequent murder of its King Joash, the two rump kingdoms were to succumb to the westward expansion of Assyria.

At the beginning of the eighth century B.C.E. Israel and Judah retained some autonomy. But after an unsuccessful attack by Judah, the Israelites entered Jerusalem and destroyed it. But the westward growth of the Assyrian Empire was invincible.

Damascus and Samaria were conquered in 732 and 722 B.C.E. respectively. The future of Judah and its capital Jerusalem looked very insecure. By 650 B.C.E. Jerusalem had been further fortified and the water supply protected by its King Hezekiah; a frontal assault by Sennacharib the Assyrian was beaten off, albeit with heavy losses of men and monetary tribute. The final act of Judah's sovereignty was played out when the Babylonians under King Nebuchadnezzar, having overcome the Assyrians, demolished the city and the temple, and carried the surviving Israelite intelligentsia into captivity in 586 B.C.E. Thirty years later Persia eclipsed Babylon. In 538 B.C.E. Persia's Emperor Cyrus issued an edict which permitted Jews, as they were now called after their home in Judaea, to return and to rebuild Orshaleem (Jerusalem). Many, however, preferred to remain and prosper under Persian rule.

Throughout all these defeats and occupations, the indigenous Canaanites and their associated tribes — Hittites, Amorites, Jebusites — had remained, integrated in subordinate roles to their various conquerors in and around the city. Aramaean had become the language of common use, replacing Hebrew, because it was the common language of the Persian Empire. Those Jews who returned from Babylon did so in a spirit of great religious exultation. In their efforts to build up not only the holy city but also their own exclusive society, they banished all foreign women and subjected themselves to the most rigorous observances and disciplines.

For the next two hundred years Jerusalem enjoyed a period of peacefulness and near-anonymity until Alexander crossed the Hellespont in 334 B.C.E. on his fantastic odyssey of conquest.

Alexander the Great never visited Jerusalem. His army — like others before and since — swept down the coastal plain of Palestine through Gaza into

The Dome of the Rock (Al Qubbat Al Sakhra) viewed from the south-west. The Mount of Olives is in the background.

Egypt. Persia collapsed, and for nine hundred and sixty years Jerusalem was to be dominated by Western Hellenistic and Roman influences, until the Arab conquest again turned it in an easterly direction. On the death of Alexander, the struggles between his generals, now emperors in their own right, embroiled Syria and Palestine. Although not directly involved, Jerusalem was included within the Ptolomaic realm of Egypt. Jews settled in its capital, Alexandria, and elsewhere in the eastern Mediterranean, where they were well treated and allowed their own religious privileges. In 198 B.C.E. with the defeat of the Ptolemies by the Seleucids under King Antiochus III, Palestine came under Syrian hegemony. The hellenisation of the Seleucids' empire soon brought them into open conflict with the Jews. A revolution, known as the Maccabaean Revolt after one of its leaders, Judas, and his brothers, drove the Seleucids out of Jerusalem after a guerilla campaign lasting twenty-five years. An autonomous state was granted to the Jews and in 134 B.C.E. John Hyrcanus became the first of the Hasmonean kings. But sectarian rivalries and disputes over religious and political issues led soon enough to civil war, encouraged by agents of Rome.

The war between the Ptolemies of Egypt and the Seleucids of Syria gave Rome its opportunity. Pompey captured Syria, and in 63 B.C.E. was approached to arbitrate between rival claimants to the Jewish throne. He naturally backed the one least likely to embarrass Rome, Hyrcanus II, and defeated his brother and rival Aristobulus, after a three-month siege of the temple, with barbarity similar to that experienced during the Jewish civil war.

Although for administrative purposes incorporated into the province of Syria, Palestine was allowed a degree of autonomy. But Hasmonean incompetence enabled Herod Antipas of neighbouring Idumea to find favour with Rome and become ruler from 55 to 43 B.C.E. With Rome's consent his son became King of Judaea in 41 B.C.E., and, as Herod the Great, acquired a well-justified reputation for shrewdness, ambition and ruthlessness outstanding even by the harsh standards of the time. By birth he was an Arab of mixed Palestinian and Nabataean descent. He married into the Jewish high priest's family and adopted the Jewish faith. His shrewdness and charm brought him Roman citizenship. The women who surrounded him were as devious, as conspiratorial and as unscrupulous as he, and, despite his intelligence and ability, his reign was one long series of crises and bloodletting. Disputes between his sons (and their mothers) over the succession, and religious dissensions, all provoked more torturings and murders. They are of particular importance only in that they formed the background to the birth of Jesus, the son of Mary, about 4 B.C.E. in Beit Lahm (Bethlehem). During his short ministry Jesus preached the redemption of mankind by

The Aqsa Mosque and the south-east corner of the Noble Sanctuary.

God, to be brought about not by the fulfilment of the Jewish Law but by the practice of love, compassion and forgiveness. His references to the new kingdom which was to come could be, and were, easily misconstrued both by the orthodox Jewish authorities and, more literally, by the Roman occupation forces. Whether the misconstructions were deliberate or inadvertent they led directly to the crucifixion. Thereafter his followers were generally persecuted by both Roman and Jewish authorities. But Christianity was already spreading abroad, and in 49 C.E. its adherents decided to abandon their remaining Jewish observances.

In 66 C.E. under the leadership of the Zealots, the long-awaited revolt broke out in Jerusalem. It later spread to the whole country, where it was not quelled for three years. Even then Jerusalem held out, and Vespasian's son Titus had to wait another year before the city's massive defences were breached in 70 C.E. The resistance was the more remarkable for being conducted simultaneously with a savage civil war between rival Jewish factions. In the end the city was utterly destroyed, save for parts of Herod's citadel used as barracks for the Tenth Legion. Judaea was incorporated into the Roman province of Syria.

A well-planned guerilla revolt erupted in 132 C.E. soon after an official visit to Syria and Jerusalem by the Emperor Hadrian. It was put down only in 135. In that year, at Hadrian's command and with typical Roman precision, the new city of Aelia Capitolina was built upon the ruins of Jerusalem: a statue of Hadrian stood in the centre of Herod's temple esplanade, and the sacred rock of Moriah was left exposed. Hadrian's refusal to allow Jews and Jewish Christians to enter the city did not apply to Christians of other nationalities, and a Christian community soon flourished.

The conversion to Christianity in 325 of the Emperor Constantine brought the first great buildings of Christian importance. His basilica of the Church of the Resurrection or the Holy Sepulchre on the site of Jesus' crucifixion and tomb is of special relevance to this book, as will be seen later. Constantine is also significant for the building of Byzantium or Constantinople as capital of the eastern part of the Roman Empire, which endured for nearly a thousand years after the fall of the western part in 476 C.E.

During the long reign of the Byzantine Emperor Justinian (527–565 C.E.) Aelia Capitolina was much like any other provincial city. But increasing pressures from the East threatened an empire which was now saddled with great administrative expenditure, with a self-seeking and complacent bureaucracy and with a leisured upper class lacking the will to dominate. Petty rebels and raiders grew more confident. Finally the Persians under King Chosroes II crossed the Euphrates in 572 C.E. and sacked Damascus

View of the northern part of the central platform within the Noble Sanctuary. The Domes of St George (El Khadr), the Hebronite, the Ascension and Gabriel, and the Fountain of Qait Bey in the foreground.

in 611. Aelia Capitolina fell in 614 and was utterly destroyed by the Persians, assisted by the Jewish population from the countryside seeking revenge for their sufferings under Rome and Byzantium.

In one final magnificent gesture of defiance, the Byzantine Emperor Heraclius counter-attacked. After several victories over the Persians he brought back the True Cross of Christ to the city in 629. His triumph was short-lived. In 633, unheeded by Christians, Jews and Persians alike, the Arabs were on the march, united in the new faith taught them by the Prophet Muhammad, as revealed to him by God.

The Rashidun ("Rightly Guided") Caliphates 638—661

The beginning of 638 saw the victorious army of the Arabs encamped about Jerusalem and upon the Mount of Olives. They had already conquered the coastline, and Damascus had fallen to the mobile cavalry of Khaled Ibn al-Walid two years earlier. The slow-moving, heavily accoutred infantry of the Byzantine legions were physically and pyschologically tired, and were no match for their swift and religiously inspired opponents. The Battle of the Yarmuk River, referred to in the Introduction, was the breaking-point of Christian resistance, particularly since its Christian Arab component defected to Khaled Ibn al-Walid.

To the Patriarch Sophronius, marooned in Jerusalem, the future appeared bleak indeed. Memories of previous sackings and slaughter must have crowded his mind and the minds of those who dwelt with him in the apprehensive city. It was after all only twenty-two years since the Persians had demolished everything, even the tomb of Christ. Already in 633 the Patriarch's departed Emperor Heraclius had taken the precautionary step of removing the True Cross to Constantinople. But after the fall of Damascus, news filtered through that the city had not been put to the sword. The supreme Arab commander, the Caliph Omar Ibn al-Khattab, was at that time in southern Syria. Sophronius, recognising the hopelessness of his position, decided that the only chance of survival lay in throwing the city upon the mercy of the Caliph. Known as the 'honey-tongued defender of the Church', Sophronius sent messengers to the Arabs promising to surrender the city, but only to Omar in person.

An exceptionally able administrator, the Caliph Omar was a man of slight stature, devout and modest. He rode from Syria across the pleasant hills of Galilee accompanied only by his servant, with whom, some say, he took

The Fountain of Qait Bey. Note the intricate arabesques on the dome. The inscriptions round the top of the sides record its constructor, its repairers and verses from the Qur'an.

turns in riding his camel. He joined his armies before the city, and, simply dressed as he had travelled, rode up to the walls. He was met by the Patriarch and his entourage arrayed in all the splendour of the Church. Having been conducted into the city, he asked to be taken to the Holy Rock. The Patriarch thereupon took him to the Church of the Holy Sepulchre, which had been rebuilt by his predecessor the Patriarch Modestus. Invited to say his prayers with the Christians, Omar declined, because he said that to do so would encourage his followers to turn the church into a mosque. He therefore withdrew a little to the south part of the atrium of the basilica to pray on the site of the Mosque of Al Omari, which now marks this event.

For the first time Jerusalem had been spared slaughter by a conqueror, and one who moreover revered the city as being holy in its associations with God and the Prophets. The Qur'an states: 'We follow the faith of Abraham, who refused to burn incense to idols, and who worshipped only one God.' Furthermore, Omar's treaty with the Christian inhabitants is remarkable for showing a magnanimity rarely offered by others towards their vanquished foes in this city:

In the name of Allah, the Merciful, the Compassionate. This is the covenant which Omar Ibn al-Khattab, the servant of Allah, the Commander of the Faithful, grants to the people of Aelia (Bait Al Maqdis — the Holy House). He grants them security of their lives, their possessions, their churches and crosses . . . they shall have freedom of religion and none shall be molested unless they rise up in a body. They shall pay a tax instead of military service . . . and those who leave the city shall be safeguarded until they reach their destination. . . .

بِسْمِ اللهِ الرَّحْمٰنِ الرَّحِيمْ

هَذَا مَا أَعْطَىٰ عَبْدُ اللهِ عُمَرُ أَمِيرُ الْمُؤْمِنِينَ أَهْلَ إِيلِيَاءَ مِنَ الأَمَانِ. أَعْطَاهُمْ أَمَانًا لأَنْفُسِهِمْ وَأَمْوَالِهِمْ. وَلِكَنَائِسِهِمْ وَصُلْبَانِهِمْ وَسَقِيمِهَا وَبَرِيئِهَا وَسَائِرِ مِلَّتِهَا، أَنَّهُ لَا تُسْكَنُ كَنَائِسُهُمْ وَلَا تُهْدَمُ، وَلَا يُنْتَقَصُ مِنْهَا وَلَا مِنْ حَيِّزِهَا. وَلَا مِنْ صُلْبِهِمْ، وَلَا مِنْ شَيْءٍ مِنْ أَمْوَالِهِمْ، وَلَا يُضَارُّ أَحَدٌ مِنْهُمْ، وَلَا يُكْرَهُونَ عَلَىٰ دِينِهِمْ، وَلَا يَسْكُنُ بِإِيلِيَاءَ مَعَهُمْ أَحَدٌ مِنَ الْيَهُودِ.

وَعَلَىٰ أَهْلِ إِيلِيَاءَ أَنْ يُعْطُوا الْجِزْيَةَ كَمَا يُعْطِي أَهْلُ الْمَدَائِنِ. وَعَلَيْهِمْ أَنْ يُخْرِجُوا مِنْهَا الرُّومَ وَاللُّصُوصَ. فَمَنْ خَرَجَ مِنْهُمْ فَإِنَّهُ آمِنٌ عَلَىٰ نَفْسِهِ وَمَالِهِ حَتَّىٰ يَبْلُغُوا مَأْمَنَهُمْ. وَمَنْ أَقَامَ مِنْهُمْ فَهُوَ آمِنٌ، وَعَلَيْهِ مِثْلُ مَا عَلَىٰ أَهْلِ إِيلِيَاءَ مِنَ الْجِزْيَةِ. وَمَنْ أَحَبَّ مِنْ أَهْلِ إِيلِيَاءَ أَنْ يَسِيرَ بِنَفْسِهِ وَمَالِهِ مَعَ الرُّومِ وَيَخْلِي بِيَعَهُمْ وَصُلْبَهُمْ، فَإِنَّهُمْ آمِنُونَ عَلَىٰ أَنْفُسِهِمْ حَتَّىٰ يَبْلُغُوا مَأْمَنَهُمْ، وَمَنْ كَانَ بِهَا مِنْ أَهْلِ الأَرْضِ فَمَنْ شَاءَ مِنْهُمْ قَعَدَ، وَعَلَيْهِ مِثْلُ مَا عَلَىٰ أَهْلِ إِيلِيَاءَ مِنَ الْجِزْيَةِ، وَمَنْ شَاءَ سَارَ مَعَ الرُّومِ، وَمَنْ شَاءَ رَجَعَ إِلَىٰ أَهْلِهِ، لَا يُؤْخَذُ مِنْهُمْ شَيْءٌ حَتَّىٰ يُحْصَدَ حَصَادُهُمْ. وَعَلَىٰ مَا فِي هَذَا الْكِتَابِ عَهْدُ اللهِ وَذِمَّةُ رَسُولِهِ وَذِمَّةُ الْخُلَفَاءِ وَذِمَّةُ الْمُؤْمِنِينَ إِذَا أَعْطَوُا الَّذِي عَلَيْهِمْ مِنَ الْجِزْيَةِ.

شَهِدَ عَلَىٰ ذَلِكَ   كُتِبَ وَحَضَرَ سَنَةَ ١٥ ﻫ

عُمَرُ بْنُ الْخَطَّابِ   خَالِدُ بْنُ الْوَلِيدِ   عَمْرُو بْنُ الْعَاصِ   عَبْدُ الرَّحْمَنِ بْنُ عَوْفٍ   مُعَاوِيَةُ بْنُ أَبِي سُفْيَانَ

The Fountain of Ala al Din Al Basir is in the left corner, in front of the Mamluke Madrasseh (School) Hassaniyeh. The Minaret of Ghawanimah marks the north-west corner of the Haram.

In 1099 the conquest of Jerusalem by the Crusaders was to be a sad and very bloody contrast.

Omar's next task was to establish the places which were hallowed by the Night Journey of the Prophet Muhammad (the Qur'an, Sura 17). After much prevarication, he was led to the eastern part of the city where municipal debris covered the Herodian platform around the Rock. The Holy Rock was at length discovered, and Omar immediately began the task of uncovering it and cleaning the site. Sensibly he ordered that no one should pray there until after three falls of rain. That day the call to prayer was chanted by Bilal, the Prophet's own *muezzin*, who had ceased to call the people to prayer after his master's death.

Before leaving Jerusalem, Omar built a relatively small mosque at the southern part of the *Haram* or sanctuary, near the place at which the Prophet had tethered his miraculous horse Al Buraq before ascending to heaven. It was probably constructed of wood and bricks, and may have been large enough to accommodate about three thousand people at one time. In 670 Bishop Arculfus, a Christian visitor, reported:

On the famous place where once stood the temple, the Saracens worship at a square house of prayer, which they have built with little art, of boards and large beams on the remains of some ruins. . . .

Life for the former inhabitants soon returned to normal. The Arabs had little experience of or taste for administration, which remained in Byzantine hands but with Arab supervision. The pilgrim traffic resumed, but no patriarch was appointed from Sophronius' death in 639 until 706. Thus by degrees the Muslims took over control of the city they knew by the simple name of El Quds – the Holy Place.

Omar kept roughly the same provincial boundaries as those of Byzantium and Rome. The northern part of the country, Galilee and Transjordan, became Al-Urdunn (Jordan) and the southern part below Esdralon formed Falestin (Palestine). Tiberias remained the local northern capital, and the new town of Ramle was Falestin's capital. El Quds continued as the religious centre.

In 644 Omar was assassinated. The caliphate passed to Othman, whose main achievement was the collection and co-ordination of Muhammad's divine revelations into the standard form of the Qur'an, which in its Arabic text has not altered to this day. Various observations and comments made by the Prophet in his lifetime were also recorded officially (*Hadith*). Perhaps these quoted below are of particular importance in appreciating the reverence and sacredness in which Jerusalem and its environs are held by his followers:

By the Fountain of Sultan Sulaiman, a woman rests with her heavy basket.

It is the land of the in-gathering and aggregation; go to it and worship in it, for one act of worship there is like a thousand acts of worship elsewhere.

Whoever dies in the sanctuary of Jerusalem is as if he had died in Paradise, and for him who dies close by, it is as if he had died in the city.

Whoever goes on pilgrimage to the Jerusalem sanctuary, and worships there for one and the same year, shall be forgiven all his sins.

Thus, many Muslims have begun their pilgrimage (*Hadj*) at Jerusalem, before proceeding to Mecca and Medina, emphasising the Arabic name for the city: Al Bait al-Muquddas (the Holy House) and later Al Quds al-Sharif (the Holy and Noble City) which was simply shortened as we have already noted to El Quds.

This theocratic condition of the Arab Empire can be said to have ended with the fourth Caliph, Ali. He set out from Medina to do battle with the Arabs of Syria who disputed his right to the title. From this time onwards the capital was to move around according to the dictates of dynastic and political control. Obliged to abdicate in favour of his opponent Mu'awiyah, who had been commander-in-chief under the Caliph Omar, Ali was later assassinated.

The Omayyad Period 661—749

Mu'awiyah was installed as Caliph in Jerusalem in 661. His capital was Damascus and his line of succession, which was to last until 749, was known as the Omayyad Period. The ninth successor of Muhammad and the second Caliph of the line was a man of exceptional enterprise and ability. 'Abd al-Malik Ibn Marawan, to whose memory this book is dedicated, succeeded to the caliphate in 684 C.E. He changed the official language from Greek to Arabic, and struck his own coins, *dinars*, to replace the Byzantine coinage.

He is best remembered for the construction of the Dome of the Rock, Al Qubbat al-Sakhra, which he started in 685 and completed in 691. In part he may have been prompted by two considerations. Firstly, a rival caliphate had been established in Mecca and 'Abd al-Malik may have wanted to offer an alternative pilgrimage equivalent to that of Mecca, an ambition justified by a saying of the Prophet that Mecca, Medina and Jerusalem were equally deserving of pilgrimage by the faithful. Secondly, he was perhaps anxious to build an Islamic shrine which would eclipse the Christian Church of the Resurrection (the Holy Sepulchre), for it is significant that the dimensions of the Dome are almost the same as those of the church at that time, while

Children play by the south 'mawazzin' arches and the marble pulpit of Burhan el Din.

the sheath of gold with which he covered it gave his shrine a most superb appearance.

The Arab historian Ya'qubi, writing in 874, states:

Then 'Abd al-Malik built above the Rock a dome and the people took to the custom of circumambulating the Rock, even as they had processed around the Ka'aba (in Mecca).

Another historian, Muqaddasi, writing a century later, stated:

And in like manner the Caliph 'Abd al-Malik, noting the greatness of the Church of the Holy Sepulchre and its magnificence, was moved lest it should dazzle the minds of the Muslims, and hence erected above the Rock a dome which is now to be seen there.

Be that as it may, there is no doubt that 'Abd al-Malik built the Dome of the Rock as the greatest possible expression of the Faith which he and his people could achieve. It was an act of sublime devotion, and we may still marvel at the artistry and craftsmanship of this building. It is the oldest existing Islamic shrine in the world. Although its design is Byzantine, its decoration and the sum of the whole is Islamic.

Let us now consider the Rock itself and the problem of building over it in suitable fashion for circumambulation. The summit of Mount Moriah, it stands about one and a half metres above the floor at its highest part and is approximately eighteen by thirteen metres in area. Beneath it is a cave about four and a half metres square, in the roof of which there is a hole about a metre in diameter.

The Dome of the Rock is a shrine which protects the Holy Rock. It is an octagonal building whose walls are 20·6 metres wide and 12·1 metres high (including the height of the parapet). There are five windows in the upper part of each wall, with two blank windows at each end. In 'Abd al-Malik's mosque all seven windows were open and fitted with iron grilles instead of today's ceramic tiles. Within the walls the Rock is circumscribed by a circle of twelve columns and four piers supporting a drum, 20·44 metres in diameter and 9·4 metres deep, in which there are sixteen windows. Upon this rests the dome, at its apex 35·3 metres above the floor. Between the drum and the octagonal walls is a shallow roof of wood, metal-covered, which is itself supported by an octagonal series of arches resting upon sixteen columns and eight piers. This provides two ambulatories for the *Tawwaf* or ceremonial procession around the Rock.

In the original building the parapets above the external walls and the drum were dressed with multicoloured mosaic with ten spouts in each wall to drain off rainwater. Doors were set in the walls at the cardinal points, with subsequently a smaller window above each one. Each door was 2·6 metres

The drum and cupola of the Dome of the Rock. The inscription round the drum beneath the Dome is from the Qur'an, Sura 17 (Night Journey), verses 1–8. The lower inscription along the top of the octagonal sides are verses 22–23 of Sura 36 (Ya Sin).

wide and 4·3 metres high, and these dimensions have not been changed. The porches above and around them have been subjected to alteration and restoration at various times, but it seems that originally they were tunnel-shaped, resting on massive wooden beams supported by eight or ten pillars. A shallow gable-like roof may have overlain the vaulting.

The columns of the outer or octagonal arcade are of different types. Some are Corinthian, others have composite capitals. They came from the ruins of the city destroyed by the Persians in 614, and their shafts vary in length. This presented a difficulty with regard to the tie-beams which connect them and the piers. It was overcome by mounting beneath each column marble boxes moulded to look like bases, but which in fact clipped around the shafts. The capitals are surmounted by blocks of stone, above which are dove-tailed together the wooden tie-beams, which run along each side of the octagon. A beautiful metal (copper or bronze) sheeting covers the outer sides of these beams. They are worked in relief, with black background, the raised parts gilded with green borders. The designs are variations of the vine theme, with bunches of grapes and intertwined and woven leaves and tendrils. There are sixteen variations among the twenty-four beams. The inner sides are painted in a rich Corinthian style, with reliefs in gilt.

The arches which these piers and columns support are completely covered with fine mosaic in gilt, blues and greens. Here also the floral pattern is varied, and, although the vine is represented, it is mixed with palms, pine and other fruit and flowers, emanating from elaborate vases or base plants. It is topped by a band of Kufic inscription dating from 'Abd al-Malik's time. The ceiling of the outer ambulatory probably dates from a much later period, that of Sultan An Nasr Muhammad about 1327. It is of plaster, with reliefs of elaborate arabesques, star patterns and medallions, painted and gilded, and set into rectangular or triangular sections.

The inner ambulatory ceiling is of wood, with sections of painted reliefs and arabesque designs, some recalling the plan of the building in which they are placed. Like the outer ambulatory, this ceiling has been restored, but not until 1780. The designs upon it are reminiscent of the Anatolian pottery of that century.

As we have already noted, the drum is supported by four piers and twelve columns. The piers have also been buttressed, and this can be seen from the outside as well as internally. The arches of this inner circle have a thickness of 1·1 metres, that of the thickness of the drum which they support. They rest directly on the capitals of the columns, and their marble casing probably dates from the time of Sultan An Nasr Muhammad, who redecorated the outer ambulatory. The tie-beams are of plain narrow wood, eight or nine

The south Door of the Direction of Prayer (Bab al Qibla). Note the marble-cased lower walls. The inscriptions on the walls above the portico read 'The Everlasting God' and 'In the name of God, the Merciful, the Compassionate.'

centimetres square. The drum is divided laterally into three sections. The lowest section, as noted, is marble covered, encasing the arches and spandrels, surmounted by an ornamental band which matches the cornices on the four piers. Above this is a quarter-rounded moulding with gilt arabesques and Arabic inscription. The drum itself is divided into a lower and upper part. The lower mosaics are of interwoven vines emerging from decorative vases, while the upper half, separated by another band of arabesque, contains sixteen windows of coloured glass with the space between them filled with different and even more fanciful convolutions of plants and urns.

Up above spreads the dome. It is built of two separate structures: an inner decorative dome of wood and an outer protective one of metal. When built this outer dome was of lead on a wood frame. It was gilded with the gold that remained from the first financing of its construction, which had been seven years' revenue from Egypt. 'Abd al-Malik had written to all provincial governors in 686/7 seeking their approval of his intention to 'build a Dome over the Rock in the Holy City, whereby to shelter Muslims from heat and cold, and also a mosque'. (The authority is Yazid Ibn Sallam, transcribed by Mujir al-Din.) The money was placed in a small treasury, a model of the projected building. 'Abd al-Malik appointed two men to supervise the construction. One was Yazid Ibn Sallam and the other was Raja Ibn Hayah. Once the outer dome had been gilded, two further coverings of felt and skins were made to protect it in winter. Inside, an ebony wood screen was placed around the rock, and brocade silk curtains were hung between the columns and pillars of the ambulatory.

The inner dome is of wooden construction and is faced with gilded plaster and paintwork in low relief. This original dome probably collapsed about 1016 C.E., and what we see today is the result of reconstructions, notably that of the Sultan An Nasr Muhammad in 1319 C.E.

We shall return to our facts and figures shortly, but for a moment let us consider this place as we may see it today, be we visitors, curious unbelievers or devoted followers of Islam.

When we enter the shrine, the heat of the day is shut out, and, before our eyes adjust themselves to the interior, we are enveloped in a cool twilight and separated from the clamorous world outside. In the stillness and the quiet, light comes softly flooding back, muted and filtered, diffused and reflected by all about us.

We stand before a parade of veined, gilded marble columns and pillars, beneath a panoply of oriental patterns. To right and left the ambulatories lead away, the turning perspectives of their arches diminishing like downland hills in regular progression. We tread through sectors of optical precision and

The portico of the Doorway of the Direction of Prayer. Across the top of the wall are verses 14–18 of Sura 36 (Ya Sin). Beneath the ceramic archway are verses 143–145 of Sura 2 (The Cow) which instructs the Faithful to turn towards Mecca when saying their prayers. Across the top of the double door itself is verse 144.

geometry and marvel at the ever changing permanence of our glittering path.

We may now move inward towards the Rock itself. Cut about and fractured, its ancient rough mass emphasises our frail humanity. From the simplicity of this solid rock, the eye is drawn upward by majestic columns across the sparkling mosaics into the swirling convolutions of the decorations of the dome. No god in human form looks down; no pantheon commands our obeisance. Only the shimmering, scarlet-veined gold of the reliefs and inscriptions above serves as a lofty focus, and the mind is free to meditate in reverence.

In his time 'Abd al-Malik employed fifty-two official cleaners, who washed the Rock with a mixture of saffron, musk and ambergris in rose water before the days (Mondays and Fridays) on which the people came to pray at the Sakhra. Incense of aloe wood, musk and ambergris was burnt upon the Rock, and the smoke was released to the outside when the curtains were withdrawn. Five thousand lamps burning tamarisk and jasmin oil further perfumed the shrine, and added to the splendour of the scene.

Below the Rock is the cave, referred to earlier, approached by a flight of steps. Above the entrance is the inscription: '*O God, pardon the sinner who comes here, and relieve the injured.*' Within its confines are two small shrines to Abraham and El Khadr (Elijah) and though it is small in size (four metres square and two metres high) it is full of traditions and folklore. Beneath it lies the Well of Souls, where spirits await Judgement Day in prayer and apprehension. Some say that they can be heard, if you listen carefully. Here also the clouds and winds gather to worship God, and the waters of Paradise have their fount. Both Jews and Muslims regard this subterranean rock as the kernel of the world, set above the bottomless pit of Chaos. In a grilled shrine nearby lie relics of the Prophet. Tradition holds that, as the Prophet ascended to heaven, the Rock tried to follow him. Here you may touch the place where Muhammad's footprint is embedded in the rock. Here also is the traditional imprint of Gabriel's hand, which restrained the eager rock and kept it earthbound.

An enclosed flight of stairs leads up from the ambulatory to the roof on the eastern side. From this vantage-point – a privilege granted to few – one has a magnificent view. Below, the Haram extends like a map. As one walks upon the roof each vista presents its particular kaleidoscope. To the north, the face of the escarpment is surmounted by the Umariyah school and the Minaret of Ghawanimah, whose flanks are embellished by small columns from the Church of the Holy Sepulchre. Minaret and school mark the site of Herod's Antonia Fortress, named after his Roman patron. Here the occupying power

A section of wall with a blank window. The inscription from Sura 9, verses 20–21, reads: 'Those who believe . . . they will be triumphant [achieve salvation]'.

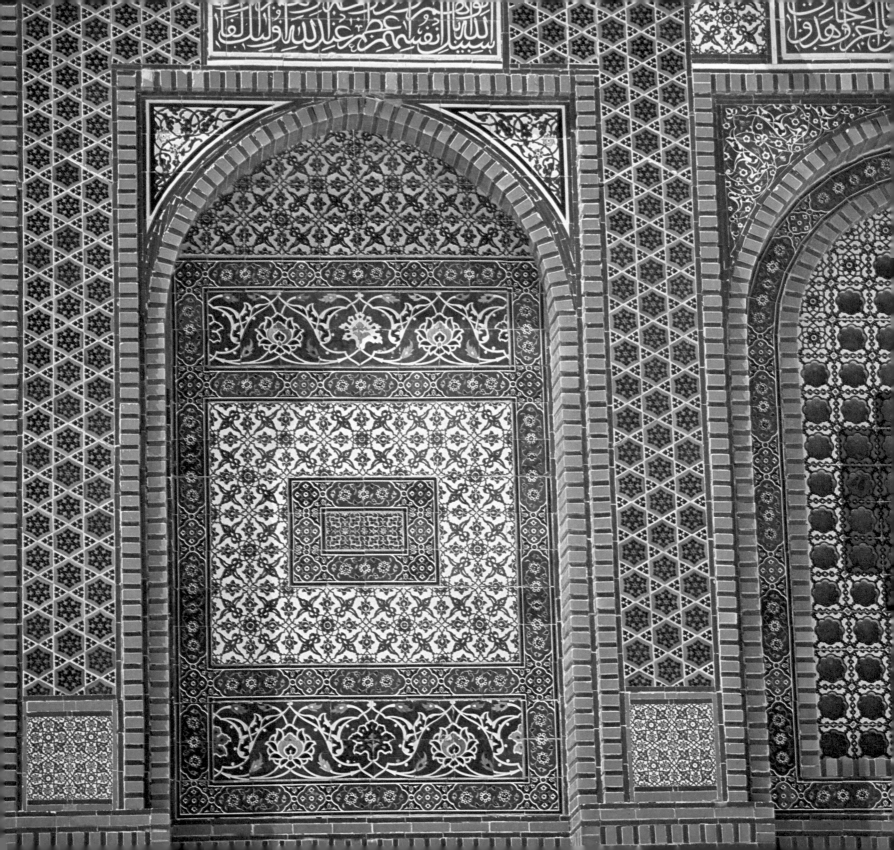

maintained surveillance over the activities of the Jews in their temple, and Pilate tried Jesus and washed his hands of his guilt before the priestly accusers. Here Paul the Apostle, taken into protective custody by Roman soldiers, made to the angry crowd, which had sought to lynch him, the famous speech of the Acts of the Apostles (Chapter 22) of the Bible. Away to the north the white mass and tower of the Palestine Rockefeller Museum marks the spot where Godfrey de Bouillon pitched his camp before his assault on the city in 1099. At the edge of the eastern city wall the beautiful Crusader Church of St Ann crouches by the pools of Bethesda. On the skyline Mount Scopus runs into the Mount of Olives, and below us the wall of the Haram now faces east, broken only by the long-closed Golden Gate. At Solomon's Throne it is said that the aged King was propped up against the wall as his life drained away, in an effort to postpone the prophecy that his kingdom would disintegrate and his temple be destroyed after his death. Nearby the Golden Gate presents the beautiful domed symmetry of lofty Byzantine architecture, and satisfies the needs of both defence and aesthetic harmony. This entrance, closed to all traffic throughout four centuries, was built by the Byzantine Empress Eudocia in the fifth century. It echoed with joyful triumph when Heraclius passed through it, bearing the True Cross recaptured from the Persians, and earlier on that distant Day of Palms when Jesus passed across its Herodian flagstones to enter the city on the first Holy Week of Christian passion and triumph.

The great expanse of the paved enclosure stretches away to the south-east, broken only by the edges of the platform, on which the Dome of the Rock stands, and the graceful arches of the *mawazzin* above the flights of steps. In that far corner lies the small entrance to the vaulted underground sub-structures known as Solomon's Stables. Massive archways of Herodian construction held the stone platform above the falling sides of Ophel, which formerly accommodated the single, triple and double gateways below the esplanade on the south side. Here, beneath the entrance to this musty place, stands the Mihrab Maryam or Cradle of Jesus. Made of an upturned Byzantine wall-niche, it has a painted dome above it, supported by four marble pillars. Tradition has it that Mary and the infant Jesus rested here before starting their long journey into Egypt to escape Herod's persecution.

The southern vista is dominated by the spreading mass of Al Aqsa Mosque, with its bright new silver dome. Beyond it, Ophel, the site of David's and the earlier Jebusite cities, drops down to the conflux of the Kidron and Hinnom valleys and the hills of Judaea roll away to Beit Lahm (Bethlehem), the birthplace of Jesus, and the desert beyond.

In the south-west, the minaret of Al Fakhriya towers above the Muslim

A window set in the octagonal walls of the Dome of the Rock. The inscription reads: 'In the name of God, the Merciful, the Compassionate. All men who believe are brothers.'

museum and the subterranean Mosque of Al Burak, now disused. As the western wall runs north, its exterior becomes the Jewish shrine of the Wailing Wall between the Gates of Al-Magharibah (the North African people) and the Gate of the Chain. Although popularly believed to be a surviving part of Herod's temple, the Wailing Wall is in fact simply part of the retaining wall, which, as elsewhere, has Herodian foundations, surmounted by later courses of the eras of Hadrian and Suleiman the Magnificent. Bab Al Silsilah, the Gate of the Chain, is a fine double gate, larger and more splendid than the others and full of Crusader columns; it was probably the Beautiful Gate of medieval times. It leads directly into the city, as do the other gates set in the western and northern walls.

Throughout its length this side of the Haram is bounded by the libraries, schools and other properties of the Muslim authorities. Above their roofs, from this vantage-point upon the Dome of the Rock, we can see the twin cupolas of the Church of the Resurrection or Holy Sepulchre, and nearby the white pointed bell-tower of the Lutheran Church of the Redeemer, which stands upon the site of that of St Mary the Latin. The minaret of the Caliph Omar's mosque stands sentinel behind the Christian shrines, and the masses of the Citadel and the Franciscans' complex break the skyline of the Old City. Having reached this point, we can now climb the metal ladder which rises steeply alongside the drum beneath the dome. It reaches up to a narrow platform, which provides access to the gallery through a small doorway. When one has edged oneself between the inner and outer domes, the sight that greets one is breathtaking. Thirty-five metres below, the Rock glistens and glows. Around it the foreshortened columns and pillars and the mosaic drum form a sparkling diadem, and from this viewpoint in its structure the dome shimmers, radiant and glorious in swirling splendour.

We must now take further note of the order of progress in the works of 'Abd al-Malik. On completion of the Dome of the Rock in 691 he placed his famous inscription on the inner arcade. Today we can read it, but with the name of a later caliph who put his own name in place of that of 'Abd al-Malik in 831 but forgot to change the date. It now reads:

Hath built this dome, the servant of Allah, 'Abd Allah al-Imam al-Mamun, Commander of the Faithful, in the year two and seventy, may Allah accept it and bless him.

The year 72 refers to the Muslim calendar, which dates from the *Hagira* or journey of Muhammad from Mecca to Medina, and corresponds to 691 C.E. At the time of the first Caliph Omar, the name Al Aqsa – the Furthermost – was given to the whole area. In time, the word 'mosque' came to mean the room

More examples of the variety of ceramic designs of the outer walls. The medallion reads: 'The Everlasting God.'

or place in which people gathered to pray within a holy enclosure. Thus the name Al Aqsa now refers to the mosque, and not to the Haram — the sanctuary. 'Abd al-Malik may well have built a small mosque, adjacent to the site of Omar's original wooden mosque, out of the ruins of the Justinian Church of St Mary. Records are scanty and conflicting, although we can assume that he ordered the building of the mosque to complement the shrine. It was built and finished in 715 by his son, Al Walid Ibn 'Abd al-Malik, who had succeeded his father in 705. Little is known of the layout of Walid's mosque, since it was destroyed by an earthquake in 746 and much of it reverted to rubble. But it does seem that some of the columns were built into the structure in the south-eastern part of later and existing buildings. It is also likely that its doors were plated in gold and silver, and that it had a high-pitched roof and a dome above the central nave.

It is perhaps worth while considering for a moment the wider ramifications of the Omayyad caliphate. Al Walid Ibn 'Abd al-Malik has remained the supreme champion of Arab supremacy and warfare. By 715 Arab armies had swept across Africa to the Atlantic, and were thrusting across the Pyrenees into France. In the East, only the rugged mountains on the borders of China finally stopped their march. The impetus of their advance was sustained by the new faith, long after the initial breakout from the parched Arabian heartland had brought them badly needed economic relief and sustenance. The simple message of Islam found ready converts among the people who recognised social justice as well as godliness within its framework. The Western world was turned upside down as this grossly underestimated force, part liberation movement, part evangelical, obliterated the empires of Greece and Rome and Persia. In its wake, it brought science and culture into the darkened continent of Europe, and by its very threat, helped to create the first stirrings of a European entity. In after years the succeeding caliphate of the Abbasids did much to obscure these achievements, but we have only to look at the great mosque in Damascus, the Dome of the Rock in Jerusalem and, far away in Spain, the gorgeous splendour of 'Abd al-Rahman III's Mosque in Cordoba to appreciate the stamp of authority and superb artistry which these erstwhile desert people made uniquely their own out of the craftsmanship of Byzantine and Persian engineers and artists.

The Abbasid Period 750–969

The major work of the Abbasid period was the restoration and rebuilding of the Aqsa Mosque by the second Abbasid Caliph, Abu Jafer al-Mansur. An earthquake in 747 had caused much damage. In 771 Caliph al-Mansur

Interior of the Dome of the Rock. A metal-covered tie-beam and capital below the arches which separate the inner and outer ambulatories.

visited Jerusalem and prayed there, noting the damage done to the Holy Places. The gold and silver ornamentations on the door were to be melted down in order to pay for this restoration; there is some doubt whether this was in fact begun under this caliph. If so, it may have disappeared in another earthquake. Such evidence as we have shows the work to have been taken in hand in 780 under the next Caliph, Muhammad al-Mahdi. From this date until 985 there appears to have been little change, and the mosque remained substantially, if not exactly, as described by the Arab historian Muqaddasi in 985. This tells us that the building had fifteen doorways in the north wall and eleven in the eastern wall. The main north doorway, facing the *mihrab* at the opposite end of the building, was covered with brass plate. The interior was filled with two hundred and eighty columns set in twenty rows.

The Dome of the Rock was repaired by the Caliph al-Mamoun, and his alteration to 'Abd al-Malik's inscription, referred to above, recorded his work, albeit fraudulently. His mother, Umm al-Moktader, presented four new doors of tannub wood from Indonesia.

After the merciless slaughter of its former rivals, the Omayyads, the Abbasid dynasty reached its zenith under the great Caliph Harun al-Rashid — known as the Upright One. Harun al-Rashid maintained a great court in Baghdad and sensibly set out to establish good relations with Western Christendom, which was in conflict with the eastern Byzantine Empire. Ambassadors were exchanged with the Emperor Charlemagne, along with costly gifts and much ceremonial, but there is probably no truth in the story that the Caliph gave Charlemagne's emissaries a set of keys to the Church of the Holy Sepulchre in Jerusalem. Christian advisers in Baghdad were advanced in both civil and military service and their missionaries reached out to India and China. The Jews also thrived as bankers and money-changers and in other commercial ventures.

However, the close of the tenth century saw a general decline and fragmentation amongst both Christian and Muslim powers. The Byzantines exploited the situation to invade Syria and Palestine, but the campaign came to a sudden close with the death of their Emperor, Nicephorus Phocas, in 976.

The Fatimid Period 969–1071 and 1096–1099

At this time Egypt came under the control of a Turkish mameluke general, Ahmed Ibn Tulun, who subsequently broke away from the caliphate and established Egypt's independence. Military conquest soon brought Syria under the new Egyptian sovereignty. But he made little or no impression

The shrine of the Prophet Muhammad's hair and other relics, beside the Sacred Rock.

on Palestine and Jerusalem, and his dynasty was short-lived. The Abbasids regained control, but lost it again in 969 to a new upsurge of descendants of the Caliph Ali and the Prophet Muhammad's daughter, Fatima. Calling themselves Fatimids, they did not recognize any other line of caliphs and even disputed amongst themselves as to which of Caliph Ali's descendants formed the legal line. They captured Jerusalem in 966 and Egypt in 969.

Al Hakim Bi-Amrillah succeeded to this caliphate in 996, and his reign is marked by its cruel treatment of non-Muslims and their property in Jerusalem. He destroyed the Church of the Holy Sepulchre, and displayed a similar lack of concern for orthodox Islam by declaring himself to be a reincarnation of God! Only a small, warlike Syrian sect, calling themselves Druze after their leader, believed in him, and to this day they await Al Hakim's return. He was murdered in Cairo in 1021 in a plot instigated by his own sister.

Amid all these political upheavals, the Dome of the Rock and the Al Aqsa were severely damaged by earthquake in 1016. The external colonnade of the Aqsa Mosque, erected by Ibn Tahir to form a porch on the north face, and the north wall were probably destroyed.

Nasir-i-Khusrau, a Persian visitor to Jerusalem in 1047, describes five gates in the north wall of the Aqsa Mosque and ten in the east, with no mention of the north colonnade. He relates that the pulpit was enamelled and that the roof was of beautifully carved wood. All this work was carried out by command of Al-Hakim's son Al Zaher Li-I'zaz Dinillah in 1022 and executed by 'Ali Ibn Ahmed, whose name was included in the inscription recording the restoration placed inside the dome of the Aqsa Mosque.

In 1033/4 another earthquake caused great damage, which was also repaired under Al Zaher's direction. Professor Creswell, in his famous work *Early Muslim Architecture*, concludes that much of the present-day Al Aqsa is of this period, in so far as the southern or Qibla wall dates partly from it or from earlier times. The main central aisle and columns and the transverse dome-bearing arches also date from this time. But, according to this description, the width of the mosque had by now been reduced to seven aisles.

Written above the central arch in mosaic is Al Zaher's commemorative inscription:

In the name of merciful and compassionate God . . . this mosque was restored by our prince Ali Abu Hassan al-Imam al-Zaher Li-I'zaz Dinillah, prince of the believers, the son of Al Hakim Bi-Amrillah, may God bless his soul . . . in the year 427 H. (1046 c.e.)

Further repairs were carried out in 1066 by the Caliph al-Mustanser, who recorded their completion on the north wall of the central aisle.

A panel of the outer ambulatory of the Dome of the Rock.

The damage to the Dome of the Rock had also been severe. The dome itself collapsed and had to be completely rebuilt in 1022 by Al Zaher Li-I'zaż, whose inscription recording this is to be found on a beam in the casing framework. A second inscription can be seen inside the drum in green and gold tiling, just above the supporting arches. Again from Nasir-i-Khusrau's account, we learn that, although the structure as a whole was substantially as it is today, there were three columns between the pillars of the outer ambulatory and two between those of the inner: just the reverse of what we now see. He goes on to describe a marble balustrade surrounding the Rock, beautiful silk carpets on the floor, and hanging from the centre of the dome a large silver candelabrum (the chain is still there) weighing a ton, the gift of the Sultan of Egypt. The roof was lead-covered, and the doors were of teak. However, in 1060 the great candelabrum fell down — during another earth tremor possibly — and this was regarded as an ill omen for Jerusalem and Islam. The omen was unhappily justified.

The Seljuk Period 1071–1096

In 1077 the Seljuk Turks captured Palestine and Jerusalem. These fierce nomads had advanced at the turn of the century out of central Asia from Turkistan and Bukhara. The weakened Abbasid caliphate of the north was no match for them, and Baghdad had fallen in 1055. Their leader Tughrul died in 1063 and was succeeded by his brilliant nephew Alp Arslan. On the latter's assumption of the caliphate the erstwhile Abbasid Empire was firmly under Seljuk control from Damascus to Bukhara, and this provided a secure and firm base from which Alp Arslan launched further attacks on Byzantium. In 1071 he inflicted a resounding defeat upon the Greeks at Mansikert in Armenia, capturing the Byzantine Emperor, Romanus Diogenes. The Seljuk Turks had accepted Islam many years before, and now these tough colonisers from beyond the Caucasus settled into Asia Minor, laying the foundations of modern Turkey. But for all his rough and illiterate background, Alp Arslan showed a profound appreciation of the arts and learning in the choice of his advisers and administrators. He died of poison in 1092.

As the Fatimid and Seljuk empires fragmented, they may have heard the echo of a call to arms from far-away France.

The mosaic-covered arches supporting the roof above the ambulatories. The inscription reads: '. . . and His prophet Muhammad is the Prophet of God, may God's mercy remain upon him . . .'.

The Crusader Kingdom 1099–1187

At Clermont in November 1095 Pope Urban II appealed to Western Christendom to free the Holy City in what the Arab historian Phillip Hitti describes as 'probably the most effective speech in history'. Europe had not forgotten the incursion of Islam through the Pyrenees. The effort to drive the Arab armies out was still being bitterly sustained; it was only in 1066 that the Normans recaptured Sicily. The defeat of Byzantium by the Muslim Turks, coupled with the fearful stories describing the persecution of Christians in Palestine and the danger to their Holy Places at the hands of the Caliph Al Hakim, conjured up an enormous threat to Western Christendom. The situation was a challenge for both sides. For the European states there was the opportunity to combine political expediency with religious fervour, while, at a personal level, underprivileged elements, such as high-born younger sons, might seek wealth and advancement, and expect to receive divine approval in the process. For the Muslims the challenge was to overcome the danger inherent in the disruption of the Abbasid and Fatimid empires, namely a reversion to the sort of tribal rivalry current before the spread of Islam. In their weakness the Muslims faced an angry, well-armed adversary, which, by the time it reached Syria, had shed much of its superfluous following to become a hardened fighting machine. No one at that time realised that this was the beginning of two hundred years of warfare, which would affect relations between East and West to this day.

Setting out from different parts of Western Europe, the Crusaders reached Constantinople towards the end of 1096 and for the next two years moved towards Palestine, leaving over a hundred thousand Muslim dead behind them. In June 1099 they topped the wooded hills of Judaea by Nabi Samwel, and beheld Jerusalem. The small garrison looked out and saw the sunlight flashing from shields and chain mail as the armoured men tramped on with measured step. Their leaders' names are well known and romanticised by legend in the West. Some were indeed men of high principle, seeking nothing but the recovery of their Saviour's Tomb and the reopening of free pilgrim traffic. Others, such as Baldwin, Raymond of Toulouse and Bohemund of Tarentum, pursued material fortunes, setting up their own principalities in Edessa, Tripoli and Antioch respectively.

Led up to the walls of Jerusalem by Godfrey de Bouillon and his captains, Robert Duke of Normandy (brother of William II of England), Robert of Flanders, Hugh Vermandois (brother of Philip I of France), Stephen of Chartres, Eustace de Bouillon and gallant Tancred of Tarentum, the Crusaders camped on the northern side of the city at the place now marked by the Palestine Rockefeller Museum. On 15th July after a month's siege the tiny garrison was overwhelmed and the city was subjected to one of the greatest

Corner panels of the outer ambulatory.

massacres in its tragic history. How very different from that day four hundred and sixty years earlier, when the small and humbly dressed Caliph Omar had accepted the peaceful surrender of the city from the Latin Patriarch. Now there was no delegation of reception, no conducted tour of inspection, no time for prayers. The carnage lasted two days and threatened even the few Christians still living in the city. The small Jewish community were burned in their synagogue and, wrote William of Tyre, 'even the sight of the victors, covered in blood, was an object of terror.'

On the 17th July, their military discipline re-established, the Crusaders prayed, barefoot, at the Tomb of Christ and other holy places, and then elected Godfrey de Bouillon their leader. He refused to be crowned King: 'How can I wear a crown of gold in the place where my Saviour wore a crown of thorns?' He chose instead the title Defender of the Holy Sepulchre. Thus was founded the feudal state of the Franks in the land of the Arabs.

Godfrey installed himself and his headquarters by the Aqsa Mosque. On its west side he built his armoury, the beautiful arched buildings now used as the women's mosque and the museum. Here was founded in 1118 the military order of Knights Templar, so called after their name for the Aqsa Mosque: the Templum or Palatium Solomonis during the reign of King Baldwin I. The mosque became a church and its dome was topped with a cross. The underground vaults were used as stables for the Templars, thus probably living up to their traditional name of Solomon's Stables for the first and only time. The small Mosque of the Martyrs became the Chapel of Zacharias and its *mihrab*, or pulpit, was incorporated into the Chapel of St John.

The Dome of the Rock was now called the Templum Domini. An altar was set up on the Rock and steps were cut out before it; they can be clearly seen today. Pilgrims soon began to remove pieces from the Rock, and it is said that some priests would sell fragments in exchange for their weight in gold. To stop the pilferage, the whole of the Rock was covered by marble flooring and a beautiful wrought-iron screen was erected between the columns and pillars of the inner ambulatory. This screen remained until 1960 when it was removed to the museum. A portrait of Solomon was placed opposite the entrance to the Well of Souls and a jewel-encrusted painting of Jesus was hung by one of the doors. A gold cross replaced the Muslim crescent at the top of the Dome.

During this period the Golden Gate was once more opened for ceremonial uses on two annual occasions. The first was for the Feast of the Return of the Cross (by Heraclius) and the second was for Palm Sunday when the Patriarch rode through the gate on a donkey, reconstructing Jesus' own entry before his trial.

The interior of the Dome above the Rock. The circular inscription around the apex is from Sura 2 (The Cow), verses 255 and 256, which include: 'God, there is no god but He, the Living, the Everlasting. Slumber seizes Him not, neither sleep; to Him belongs all that is in the heavens and the earth.' The lower panels, which are visible, record Salah al-Din's restoration of the Dome, describing him as 'Sultan and King, Just and Vigorous'.

The northern cloisters running along the boundary of the Haram were added and the small Dome of the Chain was called the Chapel of St James the Martyr.

It can thus be seen that, during the time of the Crusader occupation, religious as well as practical use was made of the Noble Sanctuary. The reverence shown in the observances at the Dome of the Rock is in marked contrast to the manner of its capture, and its octagonal plan has been copied in many parts of the Christian world. The Augustine Order looked after the Dome of the Rock with care and devotion.

Nevertheless, this Christian kingdom was an alien growth in the body of Palestine and the wider Arab world, and as such was doomed to eventual destruction.

Certain genuine attempts were made to reach a *modus vivendi*, but the quality of leadership varied considerably, and always there were acts of violence which could, and did, provoke angry response.

The Muslims slowly regrouped and rekindled their physical and moral resources. In 1140 the King of Jerusalem, Fulk of Anjou, entered into a treaty with the Emir of Damascus, since both were faced by the military excursions of the Turkish Atabeg of Aleppo, Imad al-Din Zangi. This led to a period of unusual accord between Christians and Muslims, during which the massive and beautiful Church of the Resurrection, or the Holy Sepulchre, was rebuilt in its present form. But all this was a mere respite. The Franks were living as colonial settlers, farming the best land and reaping the rewards of trade and pilgrimage. Their castles studded the landscape of Palestine, Syria and *Oultre Jourdain* as glowering reminders of the violent basis of their occupation. On the other hand, apart from Jerusalem and Edessa, far away in the north beyond the Euphrates, all the towns remained in Arab hands, and no attempt was made to cut off their intercommunication. It was a fatal tactical error on the part of the Crusaders.

In 1144 Edessa fell to Zangi. Not only was this a severe military and economic blow to the Franks, but it removed the strategic Christian position between Syria and Mesopotamia. This alarm caused the abortive Second Crusade to set out to reinforce the Latin kingdom.

Imad al-Din Zangi died in 1146 and was succeeded by his son Nur Ed Din. Cunning like his father, he was soon master of Syria. In 1167 after Nur Ed Din's attempt to annex Egypt, a beleaguered Syrian force in Alexandria remained under the command of a young officer, Salah al-Din Yusuf Ibn Ayyub, to face a superior force of Crusaders under Amalric, King of Jerusalem. Salah al-Din now demonstrated his remarkable talent for negotiation, a method which he always preferred to force. His quiet charm and courteous,

A panel from the lower part of the Dome. It reads: '. . . executor of His commands, Sultan Muhammad, son of the victorious Martyr Qalawoon. . . .'

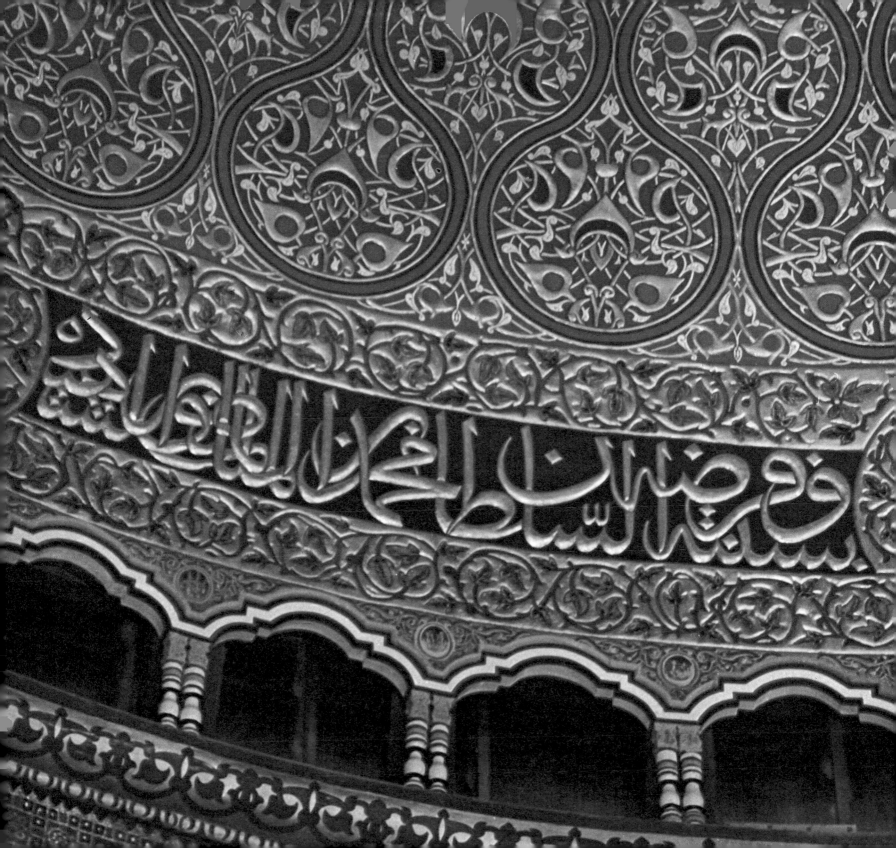

almost melancholic manner greatly impressed the knights with whom he negotiated his force's release. It is said that he was ennobled to honorary knighthood by Amalric for his display of diplomacy.

Soon after signing the truce, Amalric again attacked Egypt. This time Nur Ed Din refused to parley, and his forces captured Cairo, deposing the luckless Fatimid minister, Shawar. Salah al-Din was again second-in-command of the Syrian forces under Ard al-Din Shirkuh Ayyub. On the latter's death he was the natural successor as Vizier of Egypt. In 1171 The Fatimid Caliph Al-Adhid died and Salah al-Din was proclaimed Sultan. Three years later Nur Ed Din himself died, and so did King Amalric. Syria was left leaderless. The Christian state was torn by internecine feuds presided over by sickly kings. Salah al-Din soon established himself as King of Egypt and Syria and began a cautious advance on Jerusalem. During his attack on the outlying castle at Kerak, Krac de Moab, he is said to have averted his artillery from the tower in which the Princess Isabella, later to be Queen of Jerusalem, was celebrating her wedding to Humphrey of Toron. His courtesy was rewarded by dishes from the feast which were sent out by the defenders, but he failed to capture the castle. Its warden, a particular enemy of Salah al-Din, was called Prince Reynald de Chatillon, who consistently attacked the Muslim pilgrim traffic to Mecca and behaved treacherously towards friend and foe alike. Finally, after the breaking of yet another truce, Salah al-Din abandoned his conciliatory attitude towards Reynald, and declared a holy war, a *jihad*. In 1187 a huge army swept into northern Palestine, crossed the Jordan and invested Tiberias. Jerusalem was cut off from reinforcements from the Syrian ports. Its king, Guy, should have waited behind the city walls, but Reynald, reckless as ever, taunted him with cowardice, and thereby obliged the Crusaders to leave their stronghold and fight on ground advantageous to Salah al-Din.

Salah al-Din deployed his army near the village of Hattin between the Crusaders and the Sea of Galilee. Friday 3rd July 1187 was hot, and the advancing Crusaders in their heavy armour were soon choking in their own dust as they moved forward across the open sun-baked hillsides. By the time they reached the top they were exhausted, and stragglers were being picked off by the Arab light cavalry. There they pitched camp for the night, only to discover that the well was dry, a fact known to the Arabs. To add to their plight, Salah al-Din set fire to the arid grass, and the east wind swept great clouds of suffocating smoke over the parched and weary Crusaders.

At dawn they saw that they were surrounded. Cavalry charges were of no avail, since the Muslims opened their ranks, let the knights hurtle through, re-formed and pressed forward towards the banner of the King.

View of the Sacred Rock, taken from the eastern side of the gallery at the base of the Dome.

At last the few survivors surrendered. The King and Reynald were brought captive to Salah al-Din, together with the True Cross, which had been carried into the battle. The King was ransomed and the Cross taken in triumph to Damascus. Reynald de Chatillon was executed personally by Salah al-Din, the man to whom he had so often broken his pledge. On 2nd October 1187, the anniversary of the Prophet Muhammad's miraculous journey to the Holy City, the victorious Salah al-Din rode into Jerusalem.

The Ayyubite Period 1187–1247

Salah al-Din's treatment of Jerusalem was in marked contrast to that of its Crusader captors in 1099. Apart from the removal of the Christian emblems from the Aqsa Mosque and the Dome of the Rock, all other Christian shrines and buildings were left intact and the soldiers behaved in an exemplary manner towards the civilian population. In return for sparing all life, Salah al-Din exacted a ransom of ten gold pieces from every man, five from every woman and two for each child, but when it was discovered that many could not afford this, he allowed safe passage for all who left the city.

In his massive and masterly work *A History of the Crusades*, Sir Steven Runciman states:

At the Horns of Hattin and gates of Jerusalem, he (Salah al-Din) had avenged the humiliation of the First Crusade, and he had shown how a man of honour celebrates his victory.

While restoring all the Muslim Holy Places, he left the Crusaders' beautiful wrought-iron screen around the sacred Rock. He encased the inner walls and pillars with marble and installed the superb mosaics around the inside of the drum which supports the Dome.

His commemorative inscription reads:

In the name of Allah, the Beneficent and Merciful God, Salah al-Din, our Ruler, Sultan and King, the Victorious Scholar, Just, Vigorous, son of Ayyub, may God rest his soul, ordered the renovation of the decoration of the Holy Dome in the year 586 H. (1189 C.E.)

In the Aqsa Mosque Salah al-Din installed the beautiful prayer niche, the *minbar*, supported by elegant columns and with exquisite mosaic and marble interior. He also brought from Aleppo the famous *mihrab* or pulpit, which had been made by Yahya bin Hamid in 1168, at the order of Nur Ed Din. Built of cedar-wood, and inlaid with ivory and mother of pearl, it was a superb piece of Islamic craftsmanship.

Salah al-Din was also responsible for mosaic work upon the upper walls

View across the Sacred Rock to the shrine of the Prophet's relics. Left is the entrance to the Well of Souls beneath the Rock, and the south doorway.

about the *minbar* and *mihrab*, and for casing the lower walls and floor in marble. His inscription in the *minbar* recess reads:

In the name of God, the Merciful, the Compassionate, the restoration of this sacred mihrab and mosque was commanded by the servant of God and his agent Yusuf Ibn Ayyub Abdul-Muzaffar, the Victorious King Salah al-Din, when he conquered Jerusalem in the name of God in the year 583 H. He thanks God for his success and may God have mercy upon him.

But even if Jerusalem was restored to Muslim rule, the Crusaders had yet to be finally dislodged from Palestine.

Further expeditions were launched from Europe, and the coastline, with its important ports, was largely reoccupied by the Crusaders. The Third Crusade, under Philip Augustus of France and Richard I (the Lion-Heart) of England, which landed in 1191, was notable chiefly for the treaty between Richard and Salah al-Din, by which Christian pilgrims were admitted to Jerusalem for five years, and much of the coastal strip was conceded to the Muslims. The initiative must be largely attributed to Salah al-Din, who allowed Richard to retain a negotiating position, and to the personal respect between the two men. It is said, probably truthfully, that when Richard's horse was killed under him during his unsuccessful advance upon Jerusalem, Salah al-Din sent him two fine Arab horses as a token of his esteem for his courage in battle. Later, when Richard lay sick, he sent him gifts of fruit and snow from the mountains of Lebanon to cool his fever.

Salah al-Din died in Damascus on 4th March 1193. Truly it can be said of him, in the words Chaucer used to describe another: He was a verray, parfit gentil knyght.'

After the Fourth and Fifth Crusades at the turn of the century, the period of truce and relative coexistence continued until 1288 when Frederick II launched the largely German Holy Roman Empire upon the Sixth Crusade. It achieved by the treaty of 1229 what earlier military excursions had failed to do. His agreement with the ruling Ayyubite Sultan Malik al-Kamil gave the Crusaders Jerusalem, Bethlehem and Nazareth along with a corridor from the Holy City to the port of Acre. Frederick crowned himself King of Jerusalem in 1229, although he had previously been excommunicated. His strange secular treaty initiated fifteen years of condominium. It was an odd situation, which would have been anathema to Salah al-Din. The Crusaders had to abandon Jerusalem in 1244 owing to commercial rivalry and lack of religious zeal amongst their maritime supporters, and the city was sacked by Ayyubite mercenaries.

Now a new and terrible force came out of central Asia. By 1219 the Mongols

View south towards the Aqsa Mosque. The tops of the Minbar of Burhan el Din and the Qubbat Yusuf can be seen to the right of the arches (mawazzin).

under Genghis Khan had devastated the Muslim world north of Syria and Iraq. It was the end of the Abbasids who had managed to maintain the northern residue of their empire nearly three hundred years after the loss of Jerusalem.

The Mameluke Period 1247–1517

Meanwhile in Egypt, in 1252 a military coup was staged by the professional soldier-slaves, who had long dominated the weakening caliphate. Calling themselves Mamelukes — slaves — in a gesture of defiance and derision, they set about the final expulsion of the Crusaders from Palestine. Their young commander, Baybars al-Bandukdari, had been largely responsible for the recapture of much of Palestine by 1250, and he was now able to link up with his counterparts, the Mamelukes of Syria. But the Mongols swept on, capturing Aleppo, Damascus and Sidon. In the accompanying massacres, only Christians survived, because of a treaty between the Armenians and the Mongol leader Hulagu.

At last the Mongol hordes were stopped by Baybars in a decisive battle north-east of Jerusalem at Ain Jalut in 1260. Anthony Nutting gives his opinion of this victory in his book *The Arabs*: 'An army of slaves had saved Islam, and hence the whole civilized world, from being engulfed by the tide of Mongol barbarism.' Baybars kept striking. Although he failed to witness the withdrawal of the last Crusade rearguard in 1291 — he died in 1277 — he besieged their last remaining garrisons in Acre, Tyre and Tripoli. He forced the Mongols back beyond the Euphrates, and his successor Al Din Qalawoon defeated them decisively, bringing his captives back to Cairo in chains and festooned with the heads of their dead comrades.

As well as their violent and terrible military campaigns, the Mamelukes undertook considerable repair work to the Dome of the Rock. In 1270 Baybars restored the mosaics covering the outside walls; they were again restored in 1294 by Al Malek Zayn-ed-Din. In 1318 Al Malek Muhammad Ibn Qalawoon redecorated the inside of the dome, together with the mosaics, and renewed the outer lead casing. His inscription above the stained glass windows reads: *This Qubbat (Dome) was renovated and regilded, and the outer one leaded by order of our Lord, God's shadow on earth, executor of His commands, Sultan Muhammad, son of the Victorious and Martyred Qalawoon, may God rest his soul, in the year 718 H.*

The last recorded work carried out by the Mamelukes to the Dome of the Rock was in 1467 when Al-Ashraf Qait Bey sheathed the four doors with decorated copper.

The massive pillars and arches of the Herodian substructure known as 'Solomon's Stables' under the southern part of the Haram.

Since we have reached a point in time at which the Aqsa Mosque is substantially built as it stands today, we should now take note of its dimensions. It is eighty metres long and some fifty metres wide. Extending along the northern wall over the seven doorways, it has a porch with seven arches, built in 1217–18 by Mu'lazzam 'Isa, a nephew of Salah al-Din. There are two other doors on the west side and one each on the south and east. The main north doors date from the Fatimid period. There are seven aisles, the widest being the central one, which has a beautiful carved and painted roof, supported by massive columns with Corinthian capitals. The mosaics of the northern side of the dome-bearing arches of the mosque date from 1035 and are the work of the Caliph Al-Zaher I'l-zaz Dinillah. Altogether there are seventy-five columns and thirty-three piers in the structure, and six small columns by the *mihrab*. The columns are about six and a half metres from the floor to the top of the capitals, which support tie-beams of decorated and gilded metal. To the west of Salah al-Din's *minbar* are two small *mihrabs* dedicated to Moses and Jesus. The eastern transept contains the two chapels or mosques of Omar and of the Forty Martyrs and the small *mihrab* of Zacharia, in which there was a beautiful rose window when it was the Crusader Chapel of St John. The western transept joins the Crusader vaulted gallery, now the women's mosque (Jami an Nisa), and the former Mosque of Western Peoples, now the Islamic museum. The dome, resplendent in a silver anodised outer covering, stands at the southern end by the *mihrab* and the *minbar*, and is part of Al Zaher's construction. Its apex is nearly eighteen metres above the floor, and its mosaic work, perhaps the most beautiful in all the Haram, was the gift of Salah al-Din in 1189. Four arches, upon eight pillars and piers, support the dome.

There are seven stained glass windows in the cupola of the dome, and twenty-one on each side of the central aisle. Altogether, there are one hundred and twenty-one coloured and thirty-four plain windows in the mosque, but most of them are modern copies, replacing earlier ones.

Beneath the mosque, the vaults in Al Aqsa al-Qadimah run parallel to the aisles above, down to the bricked-up Double Gate of Herodian construction. To the east the outlines of the closed-up Triple and Single Gates can be seen in the southern wall.

Before leaving the Mamelukes one should recognise the many institutes of religion and learning which they set up in the city and on the northern and western boundaries of the Haram. These included *Sharia* (courts) and *Waqf* (religious trusts), which administered the legislation and finances of the Holy Places. Earlier, Salah al-Din had been prominent for his work in this field, but it was under the Mamelukes that the four minarets were built.

The north front and main entrance to Al Aqsa Mosque. In the foreground is 'El Kas' the fountain for ritual ablutions before prayers.

The Ottoman Period 1517–1917

The Ottoman Turks had erupted out of Anatolia in the fourteenth century. But once more the Mongols, this time under the fearsome Tamerlane, embarked on a period of bloody conquest, which seriously weakened not only the Turks, but also Syria and Iraq. They left a gruesome trail of huge pyramids of skulls in their wake as far south as Damascus. But Tamerlane's death ended this orgy of destruction and the Ottomans resumed their own venture of conquest. In the West they took Constantinople in 1453 and swept on up the Danube. In the East the swords of the Persians and the Syrians were no match for the Ottoman artillery. By 1517 both Jerusalem and Cairo had fallen to the Ottoman Turks. The lethargic, suffocating and debilitating blanket of their rule (or misrule) enveloped the Arab world. Originally their feudal attitude helped to regenerate the peasant economy of their newly acquired colonies, but a hundred years saw an end to any beneficent influence. They seemed to have neither the desire nor the capacity to run a peacetime administrative machine.

However, their second sultan, Suleiman I, known as 'The Magnificent', left a lasting imprint upon Jerusalem. Between 1537 and 1541 he completely rebuilt the city walls, including those of the south and east which form part of the Noble Sanctuary. In 1545–6 he replaced the mosaics on the drum below the dome with lovely coloured tiles, and later extended this decoration to the upper parts of the octagon walls. These tiles have been repaired repeatedly since artisans from Kashan first placed them. He also renewed six of the windows broken in 1538 and restored the north doorway in 1552 and the east and west doorways in 1566. His inscription above the north doorway, Al Bad Al Jannah or Gate of Heaven, reads:

He has renovated in the shadow of his reign, thanks to God, the Qubbat al-Sakhra of His Holy Place, the building which is magnificent and glorious. His Majesty, the Sultan and generous King, who is in word and truth the heir of the Caliphate and Father of conquests, Suleiman Khan, son of Sultan Salim Khan, famous for his generosity, victorious, renowned for his many good qualities: the son of Bayazeed, son of His Majesty heroic in battle Sultan Muhammad Ibn Othman, may God rain blessings upon them. Thus he has brought it to its ancient glory through the greatest of architects, who made it even better than it was, in the year 959 H. The honour of writing this inscription was given to Abdullah of Tabriz.

Four Ottoman sultans of the nineteenth century carried out significant work on the Dome of the Rock:
In 1817 Sultan Mahmud restored some of the external marble and built the porticoes of the Qibla (south) door.

The western arcades of the Aqsa Mosque. The medallions refer to: 'Ali' (Ali Abu Talib), 'Azoubeir' (Abdullah Azoubeir) and 'Abu Bakr', cousin, friend and father-in-law of the Prophet respectively.

In 1853 Sultan Abdul Majid overhauled the Dome of the Rock and strengthened the actual dome.
In 1874 Sultan 'Abdul Aziz repaired the wooden ceilings, the marble floor, the interior walls at the lower courses and a number of windows.
In 1876 Sultan 'Abdul Hamid II carpeted the floor and hung a beautiful crystal chandelier over the Rock. This hangs now in the Aqsa Mosque. He also inserted the beautiful Kashan tiles bearing the chapter 'Ya Sin' from the Qur'an into the upper part of the outer walls.

In the eighteenth and nineteenth centuries important work was also carried out on the Aqsa Mosque:
In 1752 Sultan Othman III used 25,000 pounds of lead in repairs to the dome of the Aqsa Mosque and the Dome of the Rock.
In 1817 Sultan Mahmud II undertook work of a general nature.
In 1840 Sultan 'Abdul Majid undertook further work.
In 1874 Sultan 'Abdul Aziz fitted new stained glass windows.
In 1876 Sultan 'Abdul Hamid II brought carpets from Persia for the floor.

Stagnating under the Turkish rule, the Levant was now unceasingly threatened from the north-west. The Suez Canal increased the sensitivity of the trade routes to Europe's colonies and markets in the Orient. Imperial Russia continued her drive towards southern outlets into the Mediterranean and the Indian Ocean. The European powers jockeyed for supremacy amongst themselves. Persecution of Jews in Russia and other parts of eastern Europe gave momentum to the Zionist movement, which sought to promote a political interpretation of Judaism within Palestine.
In 1917 Jerusalem was captured by the British, and the Turks were driven out after four hundred years of occupation. In this campaign the allies had been assisted by the Arab Revolt, led by Al Sharif Hussein of Mecca, in return for British and French promises of independence for the Arab people. These promises could not be and were not kept, largely because of the Balfour Declaration of 1917 to the Zionists, which promised:
. . . the establishment in Palestine of a Jewish national home for the Jewish people . . . it being clearly understood that nothing may be done which may prejudice the civil and religious rights of the existing non-Jewish communities in Palestine.
This deliberately confused document has been the cause of much subsequent injustice towards the indigenous inhabitants of Palestine.

Twentieth-century reconstructed pillar and tie-beams stand out against Al Zaher's eleventh-century mosaic and the restored ceiling of the central aisle. The medallion (bottom left) reads: 'Omar' (Omar Ibn Khattab).

The British Mandate 1920–1948

With the establishment of the British Mandate in 1920, the custody of the Islamic Holy Places was placed in the charge of the Supreme Muslim Council. Various unsuccessful attempts were made by the Jews to claim ownership of part of the western wall of the Haram, which had become known as the *Wailing Wall*, referred to previously. The land about the wall at this point had been a Muslim trust of houses for pilgrims, students and scholars since the time of Salah-al-Din, and eventually in 1930 an international commission under the League of Nations found that the western wall, the pavement in front of it and the houses of the Magharabi quarter constituted a Muslim holy place and a religious foundation. They agreed that Jews should have access to the pavement in front of the wall for devotional purposes only.

Rising damp and decay now threatened the foundations of the Dome of the Rock, and temporary work was undertaken to avoid collapse. The Aqsa Mosque was in even greater danger. Massive work was undertaken in 1926 and 1927. The foundations of the underground Al Aqsa Quadima were strengthened and the supporting pillars and arches of the dome were renewed. The southern wall and the roof over the nave were replaced in reinforced concrete. The arches were painted in green gypsum and gold. The new tie-beams beneath the arches were of gilded metal. Thirty new windows in true Fatimid and Abbasid designs were added and the following inscription was placed above the *mihrab*:

The dome of the mosque Al Aqsa was renovated by the Supreme Muslim Council in Thul-Hija 1346 H, 1927 A.D.

Within a month a severe earthquake rocked Jerusalem, to be followed by another in 1936. Two years later a massive programme of reconstruction began, which, because of interruption by World War II, was not finished until 1943. The eastern transept was totally rebuilt. The central ceiling was replaced by one of wood carved in Fatimid designs and colours. New columns of Carrara marble were substituted with capitals of Byzantine design carved in Jerusalem. A new stone floor was laid in the central and eastern aisles. All the work was supervised by engineers from the Antiquities Department of Egypt, and a marble tablet by the western side of the main entrance records:

The Supreme Muslim Council has restored the eastern transept, the central aisle, and front of the northern aisle of this blessed Mosque Al Aqsa, under the supervision of the Department of Arab Antiquities of Egypt. The work was begun in the year 1357 H. and completed in the year 1362 H. The Egyptians gave the wooden ceiling in the central aisle in the reign of H.M. the good King, Farouk I. May God preserve him and support his kingdom. In the year 1363 H.

A close-up of the ceiling of the central aisle of Al Aqsa Mosque. Badly damaged by arson in 1969.

The Hashemite Period 1948–1967

In 1948, the United Nations Organisation, which had no legal authority over the people of Palestine, without recourse to either referendum or the principle of self-determination, decided by a small majority to agree to the creation of a Jewish state in Palestine, providing that the refugees made homeless by the fighting of 1947–8 were allowed to return home, and that agreed frontiers were established in accordance with the U.N. plan. Neither condition was fulfilled by the government of the new state of Israel, and only the intervention of the Jordanian army prevented the Holy City, which should have been internationalised as a *corpus separatum* under the U.N., from being captured by the Jews.

In 1952 an appeal was sent out by the Supreme Muslim Council of Jordan for funds in order to undertake complete restoration and repairs to the Dome of the Rock, both internally and externally. The weight of the lead roof was seriously affecting the supporting structure and the foundations. The tiling, panelling and decorations were all in need of attention and renovation. Over 525,000 dinars (one Jordanian dinar being the equivalent of £1 or $2·80) were donated by Arab rulers, governments and individuals. Work was commenced in 1956 by Saudi contractors. In addition to money, the Egyptian government donated technical and architectural services valued at over 70,000 Jordanian dinars, and the late King Muhammad V of Morocco gave new carpets for the ambulatories worth 35,000 Jordanian dinars.

Apart from the structural and decorative repairs, the foundations were examined and reinforced with concrete grouting. The lead outer dome was replaced by a much lighter one of anodised aluminium. Some further work was also commenced in Al Aqsa Mosque. Plans were made to include repairs to the lesser domes, shrines and fountains, together with landscaping the gardens within the Haram area.

Israeli Occupation 1967

In 1967 fighting broke out again. Backed by overwhelming air superiority, Israeli forces quickly overran the skeleton garrison of the Old City. Its annexation by Israel has presented a further series of obstacles to the work of repair and renovation. In addition, excavations carried out by Israeli archaeologists alongside the Haram walls and underneath Awqaf properties, without the permission of their legal owners, are further threatening the safety of the historic structures above.

On 21st August 1969 the uniquely beautiful *minbar* of the Al Aqsa Mosque was destroyed by arson. Much damage was also done to the southern part of the building, including the dome and the decorated ceiling. Plans are in

The interior of the Dome of Al Aqsa Mosque. The inscribed panels contain verses from the Qur'an and the names of Salah al-Din, Muhammad Qalawoon and Mahmoud II. The circular inscription above the windows of the drum records the repairs carried out by Al-Malik Muhammad Qalawoon in 1327. Badly damaged by arson in 1969.

hand to make an exact replica of the destroyed minbar, but this as with other repairs and restorations will take time. Meanwhile the ancient structure survives in jeopardy; now in its 1257th year.

The Lesser Shrines of the Noble Sanctuary

Within the enclosure of the Noble Sanctuary are a number of smaller shrines and monuments, some of which have already been mentioned. For the sake of simplicity the more important ones are listed below. Their location is shown on the map on pages 4 and 5.

The Dome of the Chain (Qubbat al-Silsilah) was built by the Caliph 'Abd al-Malik originally as a scale model of the Dome of the Rock, and used by him as a treasury. Various legendary stories credit this dome with greater age.

El Kas (The Cup) is a fountain for ritual ablutions, and originally drew its water supply from springs near Hebron, twelve miles away. Beneath the Haram there is an extensive system of water reservoirs and conduits, of which the largest is called *Bir al-Warakah* (Well of the Leaf).

The Fountain of Qait Bey (Sebil Qait Bey) was built originally by Sultan Inal and repaired by the Mameluke Sultan Qaitabey in 1445, and again in 1842 by Sultan 'Abd al-Hamid.

The Dome of Moses (Qubbat Musa) was rebuilt in 1251.

The Dome of the Spirits (Qubbat al-Arwah)

The Dome of the Ascension of the Prophet (Qubbat al-Mi'raj) was rebuilt in 1200 by Izz ed Din Othman, Governor of Jerusalem.

The Dome of the Hebronite (Qubbat al-Khalili) a nineteenth-century building of Sheik El-Khalili.

The Dome of St George or **Elias (Qubbat al-Khadr)**, a very small but elegant dome built on six marble pillars.

The Dome of Yusuf (Qubbat Yusuf), built in 1911 by Asphah Salar Syf ed Din, is an intricate and beautiful small shrine.

The Minbar of Burhan ed Din was built in 1456 and renovated in 1843 by the Emir Muhammad Rashid.

The Dome of Solomon (Qubbat Sulaiman)

Detail of the drum of the Aqsa Mosque. The top inscription reads: '. . . Al Mansour The Victorious. May God rest his soul in Paradise.' The lower inscription reads: '. . . 'Abd Al Hamin Khan, nephew of Othman, may God protect him and his Kingdom and grant him success in all things.'

The Dome of Those Beloved by the Prophet (Qubbat Ushshaq an-Nebi)

The Fountain of Sulaiman (Sebil al-Sulaiman)

The Dome of Yusuf Agha

The Dome of Literature (Qubbat al-Nahawi), built in 1207 by Prince Hassam ed Din, was originally a school for literature and a library.

The Dome of Gabriel (Qubbat al-Nabi) was built in 1538 by Muhammad Bey, Governor of Jerusalem.

The North Wall contains:
The Gate of Darkness (Bab al-Atim).
The Gate of Remission (Bab Hittah or Bab el Feisal).
The Minaret of Asbat, built in 1367 by Sultan al-Malik an Nasir Muhammad Qalawoon, and repaired in 1937.
The Gate of the Tribes (Bab al-Asbat).
The Arcades built by the Crusaders, which were restored by Al-Malik al-Muazzam in 1213.

The East Wall contains:
Solomon's Throne (Kursi Sulaiman).
The Golden Gate (Al Bab al-Zahabi), comprising the Door of Mercy (Bab al-Ramah) and the Door of Repentance (Bab al-Taubah).

The South Wall contains:
The Single Gate ⎫
The Triple Gate ⎬ All sealed.
The Double Gate ⎭
The Minaret of Al Fakhriya, built in 1278 by Sharaf ed Din 'Abd al-Rahman and restored in 1922.

The West Wall contains:
The Gate of North African Peoples (Bab al-Magharibah).
The Chain Gate (Bab al-Silsilah) ⎫ A twin structure.
The Gate of Peace (Bab al-Salem) ⎭
The Minaret of the Chain, built in 1329 by Prince Sayf ed Din Tankaz an-Naseri, Governor of Jerusalem.
The Gate of Rain, or Ablution (Bab al-Matarah).
The Gate of the Cotton Merchants (Bab al-Qattanin).

Seen through the columns of the Dome of the Spirits; right, the Dome of the Hebronite, and left, the little Dome of Gabriel in front of the Dome of the Rock.

The Tomb of Muhammad Ali, an Indian Muslim leader, benefactor of Palestine, who was buried here in 1930 in the building of a former Mameluke school of 1353.

The Tomb of King Hussein Ibn Ali, the Hashemite leader who died in Amman in 1931, in the building of a former Mameluke school built in 1357.

(Also buried nearby are Musa Kazin Pasha, who died in 1933, and his son, Abdul Kader, killed in action against the Israelis in 1948.)

The Iron Gate (Bab al-Hadid).

The Prison Gate or Watchman's Gate (Bab al-Habs or Bab an-Nadhir).

Gate of Ghawanimah (Bab al-Ghawanimah).

The Minaret of Ghawanimah, built in 1297 by Sultan al-Mansur Hussam ed Din Lasheen, restored in 1329 by Seyf ed Din Qalawoon.

The Arcades built in 1307–13 by Al-Malik an Nasir Muhammad Qalawoon.

The beautiful pulpit (minbar) destroyed by arson in 1969, which had been placed in the Aqsa Mosque by Salah al-Din after the recapture of Jerusalem in 1187.

Postscript

The tumult and the shouting dies,
The Captains and the Kings depart. . . .

('Recessional', Kipling)

. . . But we may stand still within this hallowed ground and listen to the distant murmur of the busy city. The breeze in the pine trees rustles like the turning pages of history. Long years of anguish, terror and oppression have been interrupted by voices raised in exhortation, joy and triumph. The swell of ceaseless prayer for deliverance, redemption and thanksgiving has washed over these ancient stones, but, like cross-currents about a rock-strewn coast, present controversies and rivalries are traps for those who venture out alone with inadequate knowledge or too much pride.

Down the centuries, the slow decline of Man's belief in the *exclusiveness* of his own God has brought stirrings of Universal Concept and Ideal. From the fearful beginnings of his awareness of spiritual power, which he assuaged by sacrifice and burnt offerings, he has moved towards theoretical ecumenism, and taken some cautious practical steps in that direction. Knowing the imperfections of his own character, he has sought here, as elsewhere, to give substance to his aspirations by creating hallowed structures of great beauty, such as the Dome of the Rock.

At the setting of the sun, Christian bells and evening choirs join Muslim voices calling men to prayer from lofty minarets, and they in turn augment the Jewish lamentations, which cannot have their prayers reconciled at this ancient place until their Messiah shall redeem the supplicants.

As night steals up from the valley, the Dome of the Rock blazes in the last rays of sunlight: a reflective beacon of faith above shimmering walls of emerald, gold and sapphire, which stand at the centre of this unique and Noble Sanctuary.

God is our Lord and your Lord.
We have our deeds, and you have your deeds;
There is no argument between us and you;
God shall bring us together, and unto Him
is the homecoming.

The Holy Qur'an, Sura XLII

Seen through pine trees of the Noble Sanctuary, the golden Dome of the Rock reflects the sunlight in a blaze of faith.

Select Bibliography

A bibliography on the subject of Jerusalem would be immense. However, the few books set out below expand upon or radiate from the focal point of this simple volume.

George Antonius: *Arab Awakening*. Hamilton, 1938.

A. J. Arberry: *The Koran Interpreted*. O.U.P., 1964.

K. A. C. Creswell: *Early Muslim Architecture (2 vols.)*. Clarendon Press, 1932/40.

R. W. Hamilton: *The Structural History of the Aqsa Mosque*. Jerusalem, 1949.

Michel Join-Lambert: *Jerusalem*. Elek, 1958.

Flavius Josephus: *Complete Works*. Pickering and Inglis, 1960.

Kathleen M. Kenyon: *Jerusalem*. Thames and Hudson, 1967.

G. Le Strange: *Palestine Under the Moslems*. Palestine Exploration Fund, 1890.

Charles D. Mathews: *Palestine-Muhammedan Holy City*. Yale U.P., 1949

E. T. Richmond: *The Dome of the Rock in Jerusalem*. Clarendon Press, 1924.

Sir Steven Runciman: *A History of the Crusader (3 vols.)*. C.U.P., 1953/4.

Colin Thubron: *Jerusalem*. Heinemann, 1969.

To these must be added the fundamental work of Père L-Hugues Vincent, O.P. and his collaborators, F. M. Abel and A. M. Stève, and also Captains Warren and Wilson of The Royal Engineers: *The Recovery of Jerusalem*. Richard Bentley, London, 1871.